WHY SHOULD I CHOOSE YOU?

Why Should I Choose You?

ANSWERING THE MOST IMPORTANT QUESTION
IN BUSINESS IN SEVEN WORDS OR LESS

**Ian Chamandy and Ken Aber
with Howard Lichtman**

Collins

Why Should I Choose You?
Copyright © 2015 by Ian Chamandy and Ken Aber
All rights reserved.

Published by Collins, an imprint of HarperCollins Publishers Ltd

First edition

HarperCollins books may be purchased for educational, business,
or sales promotional use through our Special Markets Department.

HarperCollins Publishers Ltd
2 Bloor Street East, 20th Floor
Toronto, Ontario, Canada
M4W 1A8

www.harpercollins.ca

Library and Archives Canada Cataloguing in Publication
information is available upon request

ISBN 978-1-44343-639-7

Cover design: Eric Mok, 3C

Printed and bound in the United States of America

RRD 9 8 7 6 5 4 3

To my son, Aidan, who is the best thing that ever happened to me

IAN CHAMANDY

To my father and mother

KEN ABER

CONTENTS

WHY SHOULD I CHOOSE YOU?

Introduction: Adapt or Die

It is not the strongest or most intelligent who will survive
but those who can best manage change.

CHARLES DARWIN

Blockbuster, Borders, RIM, Kodak, ABC, NBC, CBS, CBC, Rogers, Bell, Sears, the taxi industry.

This is just a small portion of the roll call of companies that have either failed or whose futures are threatened by disruptive technologies. For those that went bankrupt, why did they fail? For those that are threatened, why do they find themselves in this precarious position? For example, why didn't Blockbuster recognize that Netflix, the disruptive technology that doomed it, was its logical future? It is obvious in hindsight that Blockbuster should have bought Netflix when it was a fledgling company and begun the transition from bricks and mortar to online.

The reason most companies are so deeply affected by disruptive technologies is that they resist adapting until it is too late. They are so entrenched in their current paradigm that they can't see the future iterations of what they are as a business. They are good at slow, methodical tinkering around the edges—changing the plan incrementally from year to year—but true adaptation is not entrenched in their business culture. As a result, they get blindsided

1

by disruptive technologies, and by the time they recognize this, it is too late. To survive and thrive, a company needs to be in a constant state of adaptation, relentlessly adopting new ideas and technologies when they come out—or be in the position of actually creating them—and not waiting until they have entrenched themselves in the marketplace.

Traditional Strategic Planning Is the Culprit

For a company to be in a constant state of adaptation—to have adaptation as a fundamental part of its culture and processes—it needs a business-planning framework in which this takes place. Now here's the rub: traditional strategic planning is the antithesis of being in a constant state of adaptation. A strategic plan is an inflexible construct that says, "Here's where we're going and how we're going to get there." For all the talk about making a strategic plan flexible, that is not possible because strategic planning by its very nature says, "This is it."

Adaptive Planning Creates an Agile Business Culture

The opposite of traditional strategic planning is *adaptive planning*. Rather than saying, "This is it," adaptive planning creates a planning framework for where the company is going and how it is going to get there. It provides a central guideline for the company that gives it direction and shapes decision making. From that central guideline comes specific next steps or an action plan. However, you can deviate from those specific next steps—while at the same time continuing to move in the right direction—as long as you stay true to the central guideline. The central guideline creates guardrails that keep your company pointed in a relevant direction but give you far more flexibility than a traditional strategic plan to bob and weave within those guardrails.

Here is how adaptive planning works:

- From the central guideline, you develop an action plan with specific initiatives.
- When specific initiatives are disrupted by a new technology (for example, Netflix), your first reaction may be, "Oh no, our initiative or company is now totally irrelevant and we are in deep trouble."
- Then you regroup and ask, "How do we use our central guideline to adapt quickly while at the same time staying on course?"

If Blockbuster had identified its central guideline, it would have recognized Netflix as its future when it was a start-up, bought it for peanuts ("peanuts" being a relative term compared to the cost of Blockbuster's bankruptcy) and begun the process of transitioning from a bricks-and-mortar company to a digital one.

By establishing specific parameters for how you are going to operate—rather than creating an inflexible plan—and baking this into your culture, you create a company that is agile enough to act quickly and effectively in the face of disruptive technologies.

PART 1

"Why Should I Choose You?"

1

Why Ask Yourself "Why Should I Choose You?"

In our first meeting with John Panigas, he was cataloguing his frustrations as owner and CEO of his company. DG Ltd. installed retail shelving and counted some of the biggest of the big-box chains as its clients.

"I know we do things differently," he said. "But every time I open my mouth to try to explain to somebody why we are special and why they should hire us, it comes out so banal. We end up sounding just like our competitors when we know in our hearts that choosing us should be a no-brainer."

Fast-forward about nine months, and again we're sharing a meal with John. In that short time, the world had changed for DG Ltd. It was now called Interiors Inc., and John was sharing with us some incredible and unexpected successes he had achieved since the creation of this company's Blueprint.

"I was having my annual review lunch with one of my biggest clients (a major North American chain)," John said. "We were reviewing projects that have been completed, what worked and what needed to be improved, and discussing expectations for future projects. Near the end of the meeting, and really just as an afterthought, I decided to tell him about my Blueprint."

John told his client that he had undergone a process to define what business his company was really in and to figure out how that would influence everything the company did and said.

"I explained to my client that the process challenged everything that we did, how we did it and what we believed in as a company," said John. "The process got interesting when we started talking about how, because we have been in business for three generations, we have developed techniques and processes and systems and procedures that enabled us to complete our projects significantly faster than our competitors."

You can imagine that if John's company finishes the store a week or two sooner than its competitors, the store will open a week or two sooner, and that is a week or two of retail sales the company would not otherwise have. For big-box stores, that can represent $1 million a week or more.

"As we were having this conversation," John said to the VP, "my son Michael said, 'You know on our signs where it says, 'Opening soon'? I want ours to say, 'Opening sooner.'" John's client was taken aback by the phrase "Opening sooner." In disbelief, he asked what John meant. The next part of the conversation went like this:

JOHN. We can get you finished faster.
CLIENT. How can you do that?
JOHN. You know how, when we do a store renovation for you now according to the current specs, it takes 14 weeks? We've redefined the specs, and if you let us do it according to the new specs, we'll get it done in seven weeks—half the time.

The conversation got much more detailed over the next hour, and when it was done, John left the meeting with $2.5 million in new business. What was supposed to be just a year-end review became the most successful sales meeting John ever had.

A Transformed Company

John didn't walk into this lunch expecting to get business, but he walked away from it with a big score. His story was so inspiring that his client didn't need to hear anything more. John finally had his clear, concise and compelling answer to the question "Why should I choose you?" and his client eagerly responded with "I want me some of that."

What a shift this was from our first conversation with John, in which he was bemoaning the fact that he couldn't tell a powerful story about his business even though the quality of his company's work was demonstrably superior to that of his competitors. This book is about the process, called Blueprinting, that caused John's company to transform so dramatically in such a short period of time, and how you can make the same change in your company to reap similar rewards.

Why Transform?

Your company may be doing just fine right now. If you are happy with "just fine," this book is not for you. This book is for company leaders who want significantly more, no matter how well they're doing now. Constantly wanting more is a characteristic of the entrepreneurial spirit, which can exist in leaders in even the biggest and most conservative of companies.

If you are an entrepreneurial leader, you may feel a frustration that is common to many people like you. You want your organization to have a serious increase in growth, but you know that doing whatever you are doing now harder, faster, stronger will provide only incremental growth. Tweaks won't do the trick. To get the dramatic growth you want, you have to make some serious and fundamental changes to your company. But which changes are the right ones? And how should you make them?

Blueprinting will tell you what changes you have to make and how you have to make them. It starts by identifying who you are at your core—at the DNA level of your company—and uses that to guide everything you do and everything you say going forward. Clarity about who you are as an organization transforms your company in six ways:

1. It gives you a strategic focus that guides every decision you make and every action you take.
2. It gives your leadership an elevated confidence to lead more boldly into a bigger future.
3. It gives your employees a focus for their thinking that makes them more innovative and creative.
4. It reveals new opportunities for revenue you never knew existed.
5. It gives your employees a sense of purpose that inspires them to perform at a higher level.
6. It gives you a clear, concise and compelling answer to the single most important strategic question in business: "Why should I choose you?"

Let's Back Up a Bit

We were out for a stroll between Blueprinting sessions on a beautiful summer day when we came upon the hoarding for an office and condominium building under construction that also was to be the new home of the Toronto International Film Festival (TIFF). It was being built by Daniels Corp., a residential developer that was known for progressive and innovative thinking. On the hoarding was its slogan: "Love where you live."

We looked at it and thought, "This is exactly what we want when we buy a home or a condo." We want to love where we live! Daniels's slogan had what we call the "I want me some of that!" factor.

Even in the most modest of neighbourhoods, we spend a lot of money and take a lot of time making our homes places that we really love. When you add up the cost of the TVs, stereos, computers, major appliances, toasters, towels, bed sheets, pictures, rakes, curtains, and on and on and on, the cost of making our homes lovable is surprising. We make this investment because our homes are our sanctuaries from the stresses and strains of daily life. They are the family bases from which so many experiences are shared and memories are created. Like the fashions we wear and the cars we drive, our homes help us define who we are to ourselves and to those around us.

So the concept of home goes much deeper than just "shelter" or "residence." Our homes—where they are located, how we choose them and how we decorate them—go to the very notion of who we are and how we, as psychologists like to say, self-identify. And to its credit, Daniels has done two things that are remarkable not just in the world of residential development, but in the world of business in general.

First, the people at Daniels recognized that what they do has a much higher purpose in our lives than just building homes or creating residences. They realized that they are far more than a company that is concerned with the logistical details of erecting buildings, such as "location, location, location," project financing, zoning laws, architectural blueprints, municipal approvals, building materials, timelines and milestones, sales offices, fixtures and finishings, and "brokers protected." Daniels knows that the homes it builds create a very important emotional need in the people who buy them.

It is one thing to recognize something as profound as this and quite another to do something about it. So the second thing that makes Daniels remarkable is that it actually operates with this deeper understanding of the emotional role of the home as its guide to everything it does. When they plan residences and when they create purchase packages for their customers, they are constantly thinking about how homes can be designed so that they contribute to having people love where they live. It is an ambitious standard they have created and have demanded of themselves to live up to in product development, sales and service.

And it is something that is reflected throughout Daniels's marketing and communications, most notably in its slogan "Love where you live." What is remarkable about this is that it isn't actually an expression of what Daniels does or how it does it, which is the traditional role of a slogan. It is an expression of a shared aspiration that inspires people, and one that Daniels fulfills through everything it does for its customers.

Note that we said "inspires people" and not "inspires customers," even though it does inspire customers. This is a deliberate distinction because building residences that make people love where they live is an aspiration of Daniels's employees and suppliers, too. It is also an aspiration of the real estate agents involved in the buying and selling of the condos, because happy customers are repeat customers and ones who provide referrals. It is almost as though "Love where you live" is a cause and everybody who is involved in it with Daniels—its employees, customers, suppliers, real estate partners—shares the goals and inspiration of this slogan.

Let's contrast this with a hypothetical developer—HomeCo—that says, "We build homes you will love," which is how 95 per cent of the companies in the world express themselves through their slogans. While the wording is only slightly different from "Love where you live," the meanings are light years apart. The slogan "We build homes you will love" is *about* HomeCo and only HomeCo. In fact, it is so much about HomeCo, it is sort of narcissistic. It isn't a statement that allows itself to represent or be shared by any of the other people who are so key to HomeCo's effort to build great homes. Because the slogan is only about HomeCo, it excludes its customers, its suppliers, its bankers and its real estate partners.

The self-centredness of HomeCo's slogan severely limits the branding, marketing and sales power our hypothetical company is hoping it will have. It is just another brag in a veritable ocean of meaningless brags. In contrast, Daniels's slogan has far more marketing and sales muscle because it isn't owned by the company alone; its ownership is shared by everyone involved in the Daniels cause, which is expressed as "Love where you live." Because everyone can interpret the line as being about *them,* the power of "Love where you live" to help Daniels generate sales is derived from its ability to make people feel they are a part of the brand. Daniels's slogan is *inclusive* of everyone, whereas HomeCo's is *exclusive* to HomeCo.

As we continued to walk, we tried to think of other companies whose slogans were memorable and made us say "I want me some of that!" Just remembering slogans was hard enough—an indictment of their lack of effectiveness if we ever heard one. How can slogans inspire you if you can't even remember them? The first one that popped into our heads was "It's the real thing." The Coca-Cola tag line passes the memorability test but doesn't make you say "I want me some of that!"

The next one we thought of was the mother of all fabulous taglines: "Just do it." Nike's grand statement fit all of the criteria we mentioned previously: it was a cause; it wasn't a literal expression of what Nike did ("we make shoes") or how it did it ("we make shoes *better*"); it was inclusive of everyone in the broader Nike family; it spoke to a deeper emotional need to self-identify and to be identified by others as someone who doesn't make excuses and just gets stuff done. It was inspiring to everyone because it made them say, "I want me some of that!"

The combination of the perfect slogan and the fact that Nike actually lived what it believed—through its products, the attitudes of its employees and the "just do it" kind of athletes it chose to associate with (for example, Michael Jordan)—made it the number one sports and leisure apparel company in the world and one of the most powerful brands ever. The magnitude of its brand and the magnitude of its sales were inextricably linked. And everything was tied together in a nice, neat, inspiring little bow called "Just do it!"

And then we were stumped.

We couldn't think of any other examples that passed both criteria. Not from anywhere in the world. Others exist, but they are so few and far between that they didn't jump to mind immediately. Not simply that, but the only example we had other than Daniels—Nike—hadn't used "Just do it" for years. (Nike resurrected it recently but, in our view, it never should have abandoned it.)

Try it yourself. Come up with ten tag lines that a) you can remember and b) inspire you to say, "I want me some of that!" Remember, it isn't enough that they just be memorable.

So, can you think of ten? If not, let's cut it down to five. Can you think of five? Okay, how about one?

We started quizzing people: give us a company slogan that is both memorable and is so inspiring, it makes you say, "I want me some of that!" Like us, most people had a hard enough time just remembering slogans. For the most part, they remembered the precious few that we could recall. But when we asked them if those lines fulfilled the second criterion, the "I want me some of that" test, they all said no—except for Nike, which almost everyone recalled and said was inspiring. When billions of dollars are spent every year creating and communicating slogans, and almost none of them can be remembered, something is broken.

The fact that this exercise is so difficult clearly indicates that there is a problem. But the problem with a bad slogan isn't the slogan itself; it is that the slogan doesn't actually represent who the company is or what makes it uniquely remarkable. For most companies, a slogan is just a superficial attempt to come up with something catchy and memorable. Just because a slogan is memorable doesn't mean it is actually meaningful to customers.

Discovering Your Unique Identity

This book is about discovering your unique identity as an organization and being able to express that in a simple and compelling way. It is about revealing what it is about you that makes you uniquely remarkable *at your very core*. It is about making sure that every element of your organization—everything you do—is aligned with what makes it uniquely remarkable. It is about learning how to stay focused on the one magical, unchanging quality that makes you distinct. And it is about being able to tell others who you are and what you do in a simple and inspiring way.

Why would you want to do all of this? Two words: more money. Many of the most intractable problems an organization faces are made difficult because the organization doesn't know who it is. These are problems that it leaves unresolved for months or years. People tell us, "We've had so many meetings on that, but we never find an answer. So we leave it for a while and then go through the process again, to no avail." Or they are problems they think they solve year after year, only to realize that no matter what they do, the problem still exists.

What you will find is how much easier it is to answer most of these intractable questions when you can articulate who you are in a clear, concise and compelling way. Whether the questions are about product development, attracting the right employees, advertising, investor relations, store location and design, incentive programs, customer service or—most importantly—sales, having a solid grounding in exactly who you are as an organization makes them easier to answer. And the faster these questions are resolved—and the more effectively the company operates as a result—the more money it will make.

The Importance of "Why Should I Choose You?"

The most important of those questions is "Why should I choose you?" because if you can't answer that question, you have no sales. And if you have no sales, you have no company. The reality is that most companies do make sales, so why should they care about knowing who they are? If it ain't broke, why fix it?

Because if you want more sales, you *have* to fix it. And if you want dramatically more sales, you'd better have a compelling answer to "Why should I choose you?" that inspires people so much, they say, "I want me some of that!" Having a simple, compelling answer will make sales come faster and easier for you than they do now.

The Apple iPod provides one of the most powerful examples of how dramatic an impact knowing exactly who you are—and being able to answer "Why should I choose you?" in an inspiring way—can have on sales. But first, a little background. In Apple's early days, it knew exactly who it was. We don't think it was written down anywhere or that it came out of disciplined planning sessions, but it was "the computer for the rest of us." Its famous "1984" TV commercial, which ran only once nationally—during the Super Bowl that year—depicted the Orwellian world of traditional computing (Wang, IBM, etc.) being destroyed by this young upstart that represented "the rest of us."

Then Apple went corporate and lost its way. A series of big-name CEOs, with many C-level senior executives and A-level internal politics, brought Apple to the brink of bankruptcy. The company lost track of who it was, and as a result, it was all over the place in terms of product development, marketing, advertising, channel strategy and corporate structure.

When it looked as if all was lost, Apple made a daring and highly risky move—it brought back Steve Jobs, the prodigal son, to save the day. Many predicted the company's demise, but exactly the opposite happened. Jobs regrounded the company in what made it so successful, stripped away anything that was "off-Apple" and started imagining new products that could be created which were consistent with who Apple is, pardon the pun, at its core.

One of the most successful of these new Apple products, and one of the most successful products ever, is the iPod. When we do public speaking, we ask our audience members to put up their hands if they have an MP3 player in their families. Usually about 90 per cent of the people raise their hands. Then we ask them to lower their hands if their MP3 is not an iPod. About 80 per cent typically still have their hands in the air, indicating that they all have iPods. What an amazing market share!

We then ask them if, when they decided to buy an MP3 player, they went down to their local Best Buy, went to the MP3 player section, checked out the features and benefits of each of the models and, after doing a comparative analysis of all of them, independently and coincidentally concluded that the iPod was the best MP3 player. Everyone chuckles because, of course, the notion is ludicrous. They simply decided they wanted an iPod and they went and bought one.

This is a far more remarkable phenomenon than it seems on the surface. Lots of products have dominant market shares, but few if any have achieved the status of the iPod in its category. The fact that so many people chose a product without even considering its competitors is a dream scenario for any company, and Apple has realized it with the iPod. Even with the most successful products, people will at least pay lip service to checking out competitive brands, if only to make sure they don't suffer buyer's remorse.

Inspiring People to Buy

Apple has gone beyond convincing people to buy—it actually *inspires* them to buy. And when you inspire people to buy your products or services, either they don't consider your competitors or you have a virtually insurmountable advantage over the competition. We will come back to this example later in the book to demonstrate other ideas that, like this one, are contrary to conventional thinking. But the reason Apple is able to achieve this incredible sales dynamic is because it has such a solid understanding of who it is, which it reflects in every area of its business.

Apple is all about changing the game in everything it does. Not just being perceived as cool, which is very important to its brand, but actually being the coolest way for its products to function in whatever category in which they compete. In order to continuously be cool, both in style and in substance, you have to be continuously creative and innovative. These two critical qualities were embodied in Apple's CEO, Steve Jobs, and through him they were infused throughout the company's corporate culture. As a result, Apple employees strive every day to figure out the most creative and innovative ways to make their products meet the standard for success: changing the game.

Does Apple have a clearly defined statement about who it is written down somewhere in its corporate documentation? Our guess is it doesn't, which is not something we recommend for most companies, but it works for Apple. The company knows exactly who it is, and this is reflected clearly and consistently in everything it does and everything it says. So whether Apple can or can't articulate who it is, its self-awareness is embedded so deeply in its culture that it reaps the financial rewards of this critical understanding. And these financial rewards start with its ability, in the MP3 player category, to make sales come far faster and easier than any other brand.

You could argue that Apple is a really cool brand and has been for years, but you sell widgets and you can't inspire people to buy widgets. To that, we say you are dead wrong! While we think of Apple as inherently cool, it is actually cool by design. And Apple was/is so committed to being cool in both style and substance that it managed to achieve this status in a category—technology—which is so inherently *un*cool, it inspired the term that is the antithesis of cool: geek.

We believe the Apple example—creating an island of cool in an ocean of geekdom by changing the game and everything it does—proves that any company has the ability to go beyond convincing people to buy, to actually inspiring them to buy. It just has to do the work to uncover what truly makes its products or services uniquely remarkable. Unfortunately, most companies are either not committed to doing the work or they don't know how. This book will give you insight into how to replicate Apple's success with the iPod—actually inspiring customers to buy—no matter what you are you are selling, by having a clear, concise and compelling answer to the single most important strategic question in business: "Why should I choose you?"

2

Traditional Planning Is Broken

Blueprinting is the methodology we created out of our frustration with the traditional strategic planning process, one that almost always goes like this: you go away on a two-day retreat (somehow it is always two days, no matter how large or small the company is or what business it is in); you grind through the same old boring agenda year after year; during breaks people whisper in the shadows about what a waste of time the process is; you go back to work on Monday saying, "Rah, rah! New plan, new plan!"; and by Thursday you are back to the same old, same old.

We have been in the business of business planning, either directly or indirectly, for our entire careers. We can't tell you how many times we have been involved in situations similar to this, either because a client asked us to participate in its planning process or because we were observing from the sidelines as a client was being sliced and diced by one of the major management consulting firms. Rarely did this process ever produce meaningful results, yet companies continued to do it year after year without questioning its usefulness. And to be honest, we were willing participants in this dysfunctional process for the same reason as the executives who oversaw planning: there was no apparent alternative. This was how it was done.

Our passion for the planning process led us to want to create a company dedicated to strategic planning, but we knew the traditional process was broken. So if we were going to go into this business, we had to identify the flaw so that we didn't perpetuate the problem.

Why Traditional Planning Is Broken

When we deconstructed traditional planning into its simplest elements, we realized it answers two questions: "Where are you going?" and "How will you get there?" Not only do you have to answer them, but you have to answer them in order because the second question is completely dependent on the first. For instance, you would never say, "I am going to buy a train ticket," and then say, "I am going to Hawaii." You have to know where you are going before you can determine how you are going to get there. Conventional business wisdom says that if you answer those two questions in order, and you execute effectively, you are on a disciplined path to business success.

While this seems logical, it has one fundamental flaw. "Where are you going?" and "How will you get there?" should actually be questions 2 and 3 in a three-question process. The question that has to be answered first—"Who are you?"—is one that organizations either don't typically ask at all, or they pay lip service to answering it, or they try to answer it in a way that is so superficial as to render it meaningless.

What we found when we really, really nailed the answer to that question is that figuring out where you are going and how you're going to get there (questions 2 and 3) become self-evident. It's like the veil lifts and the fog clears, and for the first time you really understand what business you're in and its full value to your clients.

Once we found the flaw, we gave it a name. It's called the 5 Degree Rule. That is, if you're off by 5 degrees coming out of the gate, you're going to be off by 45 degrees by the time you're a couple of miles down the road (for those of you who are golfers with a hook or a slice, you understand the physics of this dynamic). If you don't know the starting point of your plan, you can never accurately and confidently determine where you are going or how you will get there. The reason for this is quite simple and is best understood when you apply it to yourself, as an individual, first and then extrapolate it to an organization and its planning process.

Where You Are Going Is Totally Dependent on Who You Are

When contemplating all of the places you could possibly go as an individual, whether you are considering a career path or a vacation destination, you have to evaluate each option within the context of the question "Is this right for me?" But how can you answer if you don't know who "me" is? Do you want to be a lawyer or a forest ranger? Each is an interesting career opportunity, but each requires people with fundamentally different psychological DNAs. You need to know your DNA—to know exactly who you are— before you can confidently make a decision one way or another.

The same is true with something as basic as a vacation destination. Do you want to go to Paris or trekking through the jungles of the Andes? One is an elegant vacation to one of the world's most sophisticated and cultured urban centres and the other is an exotic adventure into the hot, primitive jungle in South America. They are both incredible places, but each appeals to a fundamentally different traveller. So you have to know who you are before you can choose which destination you will find most enjoyable for your vacation. If you want the comfort and amenities of Paris but you choose the Andes, you are setting yourself up for disappointment. Conversely, if you are craving immersion into a rugged and challenging ancient culture, Paris might seem a little prissy for you.

So in order to truly understand where you are going, you have to know who you are. In each of these examples—one being a career choice, the other being a vacation decision—you have to relate the options you are considering to who you are as an individual and decide whether they are in sync with each other. If they are, great. If they are out of sync, you could be heading for a career or vacation disaster.

This is why knowing who you are is so important to determining your destination. If you don't know who you are, you can't even begin to make these critical career or vacation analyses. You have no basis for making your choice, so the possibility of a successful outcome is left to chance. This is as true for a company, a charity or a political party as it is for an individual. And who, as an executive, a board member or a shareholder, would ever tolerate chance as a key determinant of business success?

Most Businesses Rely on Chance for Success!

As it turns out, relying on chance is exactly what most businesses do because they have no idea who they are. Let's take the personal examples above and extrapolate them to an organization to understand why this is so. In the strategic planning process, you are choosing a destination for your organization—where it is going and how it will get there—from among a number of possible options. How do you choose which is right?

Traditional planning says you get a bunch of smart people in the room to debate the pros and cons of each option, often on the basis of market research. They sit around a table saying, in effect, "My personal opinion is this," or "The research says that," or "In the past, we did this," or "My force of will as the CEO dictates that." They probably don't use those exact words, but with six decades of experience between us in these kinds of meetings, we know that most of the reasons given in support of one direction or another boil down to variations on these themes.

We chose to bluntly express how the traditional planning conversation goes because it exposes how shallow the reasons for supporting a strategy often are. Without the advantage of having a clear understanding of who the company is, executives are too often forced to revert to a dubious rationale for choosing a direction. This is not an indictment of executives. They are, by and large, bright people. But in the absence of knowing exactly who they are as an organization, they have no other means to make these critical decisions.

Answering the Question "Who Are You?"

The challenge we faced was that having a bunch of smart people with a ton of experience sitting around a room and contemplating the question "Who are we?" as a company is a little too esoteric. That conversation leads to running around in circles, chasing your tail.

Luckily, around the same time we were contemplating creating a "Who are you?" company, we started having a conversation about the question "Why should I choose you?" The more we thought about it, the more we realized it is actually the single most important strategic question in business. On the surface, it appears to be a marketing and sales question—and it is—but it is also so much more when you consider some of its hundreds or even thousands of variations, such as:

Why should I work for you or continue working for you?
Why should I invest in you?
Why should I be on your board?
Why should I give you a loan?
Why should I attend your meeting?
Why should I answer your email?
Why should I merge with you or be acquired by you?

Why should I be your strategic partner?

Why should I trust your company?

Why should I approve your proposal?

As your supplier, why should I give you special treatment?

All of these questions are variations of "Why should I choose you?" but none of them are directly related to marketing and sales. They each relate to a different part of the company, such as HR, finance, product development/research and development, corporate strategy, operations, administration and purchasing.

For instance, a clear, concise and compelling answer to the question "Why should I invest in you?" will have a significant impact on how you raise money if you are a start-up; shape how you write your business plan and your prospectus; guide how you construct the story you tell potential investors, both verbally and in how you prepare your PowerPoint presentation; and influence the design and copywriting of the collateral materials you leave with your prospects. It will even have a material impact on your valuation because it will help you determine the *full* value of your product or service.

A clear, concise and compelling answer to the question "Why should I work for you?" for an HR manager will have a significant impact on how you position executive searches; how you write online and off-line recruiting ads; how you interview people, the questions you ask them and the answers you expect to hear; how you design your retention and reward policies; and how you determine whether or not you want to retain employees who are being recruited by other companies.

We realized that a clear, concise and compelling answer to the question "Why should I choose you?" *would shape every area of your business.* We discovered two additional things when we really, really nailed the answer to that question: it could always be done in seven words or less and it also answered the question "Who are you?"

Two seemingly different questions—"Why should I choose you?" and "Who are you?"—have exactly the same answer . . . in seven words or less. This isn't surprising, because if you have a compelling answer to the question "Why should I choose you?" you really should know who "you" are. The conversation around the question "Why should I choose you?" is far more tangible than trying to answer the question "Who are you?" So the question "Why should I choose you?" became the doorway to answering "Who are you?"

Because your seven words or less answer the question "Who are you?" it is the articulation of your corporate DNA (or your organizational DNA if you are a charity, academic institution, government body or political party). The magic of knowing your DNA is that you can use it to guide everything you do and say.

Let's take a look at Interiors Inc., the retail shelving company, and a few areas in which its DNA—"Opening sooner"—guides everything it does and says.

> **Planning.** Because all of his clients desperately wanted John to fulfill his "Opening sooner" promise, he was able to demand a seat at the planning table for the first time. This gave him more say in how the overall project would be executed, and it gave him the opportunity to make suggestions at the planning stage that would shorten the construction process. Clients agreed to give him a seat at the planning table because it was in their best interest to have John live up to his "Opening sooner" promise.

> **Culture.** As with most companies, Interiors' culture developed organically. Once John knew his ultimate goal—"Opening sooner"—he was able to foster an even more effective culture *by*

design. This included instilling in his people, and rewarding them for, a greater sense of urgency, greater individual ownership of the overall project and a reduction in procrastination. He also redefined his hiring process because he became very clear about the ideal characteristics of an employee who would deliver on "Opening sooner." The ability to articulate the goal planted in the brains of his employees what their mission was during every moment of every day and compelled them to work more efficiently and effectively.

Sales Story. Interiors completely rewrote its sales story to incorporate all of the processes, systems, procedures and techniques it used to get finished faster. It had always been doing these things, but only by looking at its business through the lens of "Opening sooner" could it recognize the things it was doing intuitively and articulate them in a story that was convincing to construction managers. The introduction to the sales story—opening sooner—created the context that allowed Interiors' prospects to say to themselves, as they were listening to each part of the sales story, "Yes, I see how that feature or detail contributes to getting finished faster." "Opening sooner" became the filter through which prospects listened to, and made sense of, Interiors' story.

Project Management. This function was almost always handled by the client itself or a dedicated project management company. Interiors developed its own project management system to track the progress and reporting of its work for its client. This gave Interiors more control over the timing and execution of its projects, and allowed it to deliver more value to the client and the project management company. Even though project management was somebody else's responsibility, it was in Interiors' best interest to do this extra bit of work because it made the project go more quickly and be more profitable. And when a client didn't have any project management capability, Interiors was able to fulfill that role for an extra fee.

Innovation. An unintended outcome of his staff embracing the Blueprint was that the company became more innovative and creative. If John had asked his staff to be more innovative and creative, they would've stared back at him with puzzled looks, either because they didn't know how to do it or they didn't feel it was part of their job. But when they know that their ultimate goal is opening sooner, they are naturally compelled to think of ways to make that happen because it is so specific and so inspiring for them. Interiors created a formal infrastructure for collecting innovative ideas from its employees and implementing them into its workflow and training.

The simple, essential logic that your corporate DNA can guide everything you do and say is the foundation upon which Blueprinting, and this book, is built. Know your company's DNA and you can look at every part of your business and determine whether or not it's aligned with who you are at your core. Know your DNA and you can determine everything you should and shouldn't say about your business in order to make it a magnet for customers, the best talent, investment and the most valuable strategic partners. Know your DNA and you will have your unique answer to the single most important strategic question in business: "Why should I choose you?" If you have a clear, concise and compelling answer to this question, the success of your business will lie solely in the quality of your execution.

The previous paragraph introduces the three elements of a Blueprint: the Core Proposition, the Business Architecture and the Core Story.

Core Proposition. The seven words or less that articulate your corporate or organizational DNA. It answers the questions "Who are you?" and "Why should I choose you?"

Business Architecture. We define your Business Architecture as everything you do and how you do it. This is a very broad definition in that it encompasses the entire substance of the company. Using this definition of Business Architecture allows us to use your Core Proposition to guide everything you do.

Core Story. Your Core Story contains all of the high-level information on the organization that guides everything it says, both externally (for example, marketing and sales, government relations, public relations, investor relations) and internally (such as employee relations). As with your Business Architecture, the development of your Core Story is guided by your Core Proposition.

To borrow a metaphor from Douglas Hofstadter, author of *Gödel, Escher, Bach,* the three components of the Blueprint are like the stone from which all the shadows of the organization are cast.

PART 2

No Pain, No Gain

3

Core Proposition

Uncovering Your Company's Universal Value

An organization's seven words or less define "who" it is at its very core. That is why we call it the Core Proposition. And that is why we say it articulates a company's DNA, just as at the very core of who we are as living beings is our DNA.

Not only does our DNA define virtually everything about who we are—the colour of our hair and eyes, our height, our skin colour and even, to a degree, our personalities—it also guides the future development of everything in our bodies. It determines when and how we slough off skin and replace it with new. It controls the repair of damaged organs and it even charts the progress of diseases, such as cancer, that can take our lives.

An organization's DNA acts the same way. It determines who the organization is, everything it does and everything it says. The paradox here is that 95 per cent of organizations don't have the foggiest idea about their DNA. So how, you can ask, can an organization operate according to its DNA when it doesn't even know what it is?

Every organization's DNA exists within its culture, which is determined by the collective thoughts, beliefs and behaviours of every employee, from the most senior executives to the newest entry-level recruits. This is true of companies, charities, governments and political parties, countries, provinces, cities, non-governmental organizations (NGOs), universities, hospitals and any other kind of organization you can imagine. But not only does an organization's DNA exist within its culture, it also exists in each individual employee. The more strongly the employee has been indoctrinated into the culture of the organization, the deeper will be his or her understanding of the DNA, even if it is completely subconscious.

Real DNA works the same way. All of the cells in your body contain the same DNA. So your entire body has just one unique DNA profile, but that profile is contained—in its entirety—inside every individual cell. You don't need to read your whole body to define your particular DNA. All you have to do is look in one cell.

To say you can do the same thing with a company is to stretch the DNA metaphor a little too far. While it is definitely possible to define a company's DNA in seven words or less from the knowledge of just one person—especially if that person is as dominant in defining a company's culture as Steve Jobs was at Apple—it is risky. But what we've proven over and over again in more than 200 Blueprints is that you can do it with a very small group of people.

Who Determines the DNA?

When we Blueprint an organization, we allow up to four decision makers to take part in the process, but no more. Why four? Because we've learned from experience that a bigger group doesn't add quality to the conversation and doesn't make the outcome any more accurate. All it does is expand conversations and slow down the process.

At this point, we know many of you will be skeptical about what we are saying. One of our clients has 55,000 employees. How can just four people—or fewer—define the DNA of such a large organization? It's a fair question. Our process flies in the face of conventional thinking. This skepticism was exhibited no more dramatically (for us, anyway) than in a phone call with a university chancellor just prior to his participation in the first Blueprint session for his institution. He said, "I fundamentally disagree with the underlying principles of your process. It's not going to work and I'm not going to show up." After some more conversation, he agreed to participate. By the end of the first session, he was a convert and was telling us about organizations he knew of that needed a Blueprint.

It is common in the business community to believe that the way you define an organization is by asking as many employees as possible what they think it is, aggregating that information, analyzing it for commonalities and then coming up with one grand statement or paragraph—or sometimes dozens of paragraphs—that crystallizes the definition.

Underlying this process of consensus is a belief that you have to include as many people as possible in order to get them to buy in. But reality proves that this rarely works. Just examine the vision statements, mission statements and explanations of just about any company and you will find nothing more than a confusing mishmash of business speak and buzzwords. The final proof—the nail in the coffin—of the ineffectiveness of this process is that when you show employees of the company the outcome, they usually just roll their eyes.

This is true because the process of consultation reveals only a superficial understanding of what the company truly is at its core. This is not to say that the people consulted have a superficial understanding of who the company is; rather, the *process* is so superficial it can't draw from them the depth, richness and relevance of what the company does and the impact on the customer.

So if you get everybody's input and then produce crap, which is too often the case, everybody who gave input looks at it and says, "I know I was a part of the process, but what a pile of crap they made out of it."

Going Deep Is the Only Option

Getting to a company's DNA—to what truly makes it uniquely remarkable—is surprisingly difficult. It requires a process that is the exact opposite of superficial. It requires a deep dive into the psyche of the organization, which is why almost all of our clients describe Blueprinting as psychotherapy for the company. It isn't enough to investigate and ask questions and challenge answers. You have to challenge and challenge and challenge, and when you think you've challenged enough, you have to challenge and challenge and challenge until you go a few layers deeper.

When we Blueprinted the Toronto International Film Festival (TIFF), one of its senior executives said, "We've undergone these kinds of processes before, but Blueprinting went about six layers deeper." We don't say this to be immodest about our process, but to point out how deep you have to dive in order to get to what an organization truly is at its core.

You have to go this deep because there are two dynamics working against each other in most companies. The first is a positive force, which is the willpower of the company's DNA to guide the organization effectively, although unconsciously, because nobody actually knows what the DNA is. Since it exists individually in the employees and collectively in the culture of the company, the DNA is trying valiantly to do its good work, even if it can't be articulated by anyone in the company.

The second dynamic is a negative force, which is all of the illusion and delusion the company has built up around itself over the years—or even over just weeks and months if the company is a start-up. The illusion and delusion happen because people are struggling to articulate where the company is going and why, but they have no solid basis for their conclusions because they don't know who the company is. So they come up with phrases that either sound clever, pander to the customer or make them feel good about themselves. These inaccurate statements drive a negative feedback loop: the company doesn't know who it is, which creates muddy thinking, which in turn is used to miscommunicate who the company is. As this happens over and over again, the articulation of who the company is drifts farther and farther away from its DNA.

Over time, the company comes to see itself as something that is entirely different from its DNA. You see this most dramatically in mission and vision statements, which we believe to be a complete waste of time, energy and money. They are nothing more than an exercise in corporate narcissism; companies turn to them in a struggle to express who they are and what they stand for in the most baffling of corporate gobbledygook. In our experience, there is nothing that gets people's eyes rolling more than the terms *vision statement* and *mission statement*. But while missions and visions are the most high-profile expressions of illusion and delusion that a company has built up around itself over the years, you can usually also find examples running all through its marketing and sales materials and its website.

Stripping Away Illusions About the Company

In order to get deep enough into the psyche of the company to reveal its DNA, especially in seven words or less, you need to undergo the soul-searching, gut-wrenching, emotion-sapping process of stripping away those "truths" about your organization that you hold to be self-evident, which are actually just illusion. Sorry to be so brutal about it, but it's true.

This is a process that can almost never be taken on internally without outside help because everyone who participates in it will have drunk the corporate Kool-Aid to some degree or another, even if they think they haven't. This insider knowledge hinders participants from seeing the fallacies in the corporate beliefs, plans and actions. On top of that, you have two psychosocial dynamics that make the amount of challenging it takes to reveal a Core Proposition virtually impossible when only insiders are involved:

Politics. The interpersonal dynamics of the peers who are participating in the process. There are silent—and not so silent—agreements, fears and agendas that exist between the participants that hinder their ability to speak openly and honestly about the company and its sacred cows. What you get is a conversation that operates at about 25 per cent of the frankness that is required to make the deep dive.

Power. Power dynamics exist in the sessions because there are usually participants of different rank involved in the conversation. If the CEO makes a bold but inaccurate statement about the company, how far will his or her subordinates go in challenging that statement before they fear their status in the organization and their careers are in jeopardy?

The process needs to be moderated by strong outsiders who are indifferent to both the political and power dynamics of the group. The outsiders, no matter who they are, need to have the courage to stand up to that CEO and challenge what he or she said until it is either proven correct or discarded. Whether the CEO's assertion is retained or rejected, the right thing is done and there is no compromise as a result of the power dynamic. The outsiders need to have only one goal in mind: drilling down to the core of the company and damn the torpedoes.

Why Seven Words or Less?

It became obvious to us that if we believe that traditional planning is broken and "Why should I choose you?" is by far the most important strategic question in business, the new planning process we were creating had to be built around its answer. But how do we answer that question without lapsing back into vision and mission statement–style verbiage, with all of the lack of inspiration and direction it creates?

The answer came from a happy trend we spotted in the early stages of Blueprinting. Every time we got to the aha moment where everyone in the room said, "Yes! That's exactly who we are!" it was expressed in seven words or less. So after a while we took the hint and just declared that the answer always had to be expressed in seven words or less.

From that point on, we were constantly asked why seven words and not five or nine or 14? Our initial answer is "Why not?"

Before you dismiss "Why not?" as nothing more than an argumentative non-answer, think about it for a second. Why can't you just demand that the answer be that simple rather than falling into the trap of traditional business thinking, which is to layer on complexity after complexity until nobody understands what is being said? Don't waste time with quantitative proofs or qualitative rationalizations. Just declare that seven words or less is enough, and then get into action.

But it goes deeper than that. It has to be just long enough to express a cogent thought. If you think seven words is too short, bear in mind that many of our clients can do it in just two ("opening sooner"). Second, it has to be short enough to instill a discipline on the discovery process so that you don't stop working at it until you truly have what makes you uniquely remarkable. Setting a standard that is exceptionally concise forces you to really think it through and not give up once you are "close enough." This is a pass/fail process with nothing in between. There is no room for compromise.

Finally, it has to be short enough to meet three additional important criteria:

Easy to understand. If the definition of who you are is restricted to seven words or less, it will be very difficult for you to inject the kinds of words and phrases that professional and amateur vision and mission statement developers love to use. No room for tortured clichés such as "new paradigm" or "proactively implementing 360" or "world leadership in customer service." As the great violinist Isaac Stern said about John Lennon, no wasted notes. Without the ability to confuse things, you are left with a simple statement that is easy for everyone to understand. And if it is immediately understandable, you have laid the foundation for its most powerful benefit: its ability to guide and inspire.

Easy to remember. If who you are is expressed in seven words or less, making it easy to understand, it will also be easy for everyone inside and outside of your organization to remember. In the third session of the Blueprint we were doing, the CEO asked us when we were going to work on mission and vision. We explained to him why we don't believe in them. When he got angry about this, we asked him to tell us his vision statement. He said he couldn't remember it verbatim, so he would ask his assistant to print it out and bring it to the meeting. We told him that that wouldn't be necessary; paraphrasing it would be fine. He couldn't do that, either. We looked around the room and asked if anyone could paraphrase the mission statement for us. No one could. So we turned back to the CEO and asked him why he was so intent on creating a mission statement when nobody in the organization knew what it was, let alone used it to guide how they did their work. When your Core Proposition is declared in seven words or less, it is easy to remember.

Easy to repeat. If everyone can understand and remember who you are, they can talk about you convincingly to others. As we will see later, this means you have the opportunity to transform anyone inside and outside your organization into a brand and sales evangelist. Everyone will be able to tell your story accurately, but in their own words, so that it comes out naturally, not as a script.

Uncovering Your Core Proposition

On the one hand, there is nothing complex or sophisticated about how we uncover a company's Core Proposition (its seven words or less). When we talk about a Core Proposition determining your Business Architecture and shaping your Core Story, it makes the process sound linear. The reality is that we jump right into your Business Architecture and deconstruct it, examining and challenging all of its material parts and how they fit together. The colloquial way we describe the process is: we tear the company apart so that it is in pieces on the table, at some point in the conversation the Core Proposition pops out, we bulletproof it and then we reassemble the company around the Core Proposition.

When the Core Proposition pops out, one of three things happens:

Everybody recognizes it in one of those aha moments. If everybody recognizes it at the same time, they usually feel it physically and emotionally, as well as getting it conceptually.

We recognize it and our clients don't. If only we recognize it immediately and our clients don't, then we go through a process of leading them to see that this is their Core Proposition. When they come to see it as we do, they usually feel it physically and emotionally, as well as getting it conceptually.

Nobody recognizes it in the moment. If nobody recognizes it in the moment, the expression will usually force its way back into the conversation over and over again as if it has a will of its own. It's fighting for its life, and it's not going to let the temporary blindness of any of the participants, including us, thwart its efforts to live. When we all come to see it, finally, we usually feel it physically as well as getting it conceptually.

It must be pretty obvious by now that this thinking/feeling dynamic is critical to the recognition of the Core Proposition. We are often asked how we know when it's right. We know we are on the right path when everyone in the room *thinks* it's right and *feels* it's right. Everyone. There is never a vote. There is never anyone left out of the agreement. At this point, we put the proposed Core Proposition through a rigorous bulletproofing process to make sure it resonates with all stakeholders, a process we will explain later in the book.

We were doing a Blueprint with Navigator, a company that helps clients solve the most difficult of problems (such as managing crises). For two sessions one of the participants kept saying that the Core Proposition did not include his practice within the company. In a situation like this, we have to be very careful. On the one hand, we want to try to get him to see how his practice *does* fit into the Core Proposition. But on the other hand, we really, really have to listen to his objections so that he doesn't get bullied into agreeing. As it turns out, he was right: we were close, but not bang on. When we finally got to what was really at the core of his objection, a new six-word phrase popped out that was even stronger than the one we had been working with. He immediately said he could see his practice inside of that expression and that it *felt* right. Everyone else said they *thought* and *felt* it was a better expression for the rest of the company.

The Importance of the "Thinking/Feeling" Thing

When we get dismissed by academics at business schools, it is often because of our conviction that this thinking/feeling thing is the proof of the accuracy of the Core Proposition. They believe there must be hard data—either quantitative, in the form of market numbers, or qualitative, in the form of employee polling—to prove it's true. But there's another proof that has manifested itself over and over. When we go back to a company's employees, investors, strategic partners, suppliers or board members and say, "This is who the company is," their reaction is always, "Yeah, that's it . . . but I always knew that!"

Frankly, it's a little frustrating for us, having worked so hard to define the company in seven words or less, to have somebody say, "I always knew that!" But the reality is, they *did* always know it because the DNA of an organization is contained within every individual and within the culture of the organization. And when it's captured properly, it is recognized, felt and embraced by every individual in the organization.

What We Talk About to Reveal the Core Proposition

We said earlier in this chapter that the way we uncover the Core Proposition is by getting people to talk, and then it just pops out. But there are two questions we explore in great depth in order to get the Core Proposition:

What does the company really do as opposed to what it thinks it does?
This conversation will not only reveal what business the company is *really* in, it will also uncover the underlying logic of why it is in that business and the value it brings to stakeholders. We call this the organization's Core Logic.

How does the Core Logic satisfy a deep emotional need? When we evaluate the value the business brings to its stakeholders, we identify the deep emotional need that is being satisfied by the product or service. The Core Logic has to resonate at a deep emotional level. This Emotional Resonance is usually revealed in a conversation about the customer, and then we expand it to all other stakeholder groups to make sure it resonates with them, too.

You have to address these two questions in tandem. If the Core Logic doesn't resonate at a deep emotional level with all stakeholders, it isn't the right Core Logic.

Core Logic (What Do You *Really* Do?)

This question is all about the basic logic of your business. What are all the things you do? How do they fit together in one nice, neat-and-tidy little package? And what tangible problem does that solve for the client?

The way to answer this question is to jump right into the architecture of the business, examining all of its parts and how they relate to each other, tearing them apart and putting them back together again. This is the most frustrating stage of the Blueprint for clients, because everything they have worked so hard to create and build is questioned mercilessly. Because the business is the product of their intellect, blood, sweat and tears, it feels like they are being challenged personally. But while it may feel that way, it's not actually true, because the business is almost always at least sound—it just needs to be realigned to a greater or lesser degree. So in this deconstruction of the business, which is a fundamental part of the Blueprint process, what survives lives to see another day and what doesn't is cast aside. It is a heartless, Darwinian process, but an effective one.

What almost always emerges is that the client is in a different business than it thought. The business that is uncovered—the *real* business—is simpler (easier to explain and easier to understand), more robust and delivers far more value. The new business may even do exactly the same thing as the old one, but its purpose is articulated differently, in a way that captures what it's really doing. Or it could require some serious changes in its Business Architecture to align it with the business it is really in. While the process of getting there can be difficult, the feeling of relief and even exhilaration the client feels at the end is palpable. It's actually what the client always wanted to be. But it just couldn't figure out how to get there, or how to express its purpose as powerfully as it had imagined.

What They Really Do

Let's go deeper into the story about Interiors Inc., the retail shelving company, to discover what an organization really does. When a retailer builds a new big-box store, our client erects all of the rack shelving. When it is done, the store opens. We led the senior team through a conversation to reveal what business they were really in. As with most clients, it involved two or three hours of us constantly saying, "Bull——!" because what they thought was substantial differentiation was really just rhetoric, banalities and generic services. Our client knew what *category* it was in—the installation of retail shelving—but didn't know what business it was in relative to its competitors.

The conversation got interesting when the client talked about how it had been in business for three generations, whereas most of its competitors had been in business for only five to ten years. Over the course of those three generations, it had done everything in the world of store construction except build the actual buildings themselves. It had helped companies with their location strategies, with choosing specific locations, with project management and with installing the shelving. This rich and extensive background of experience led it to develop techniques, processes, systems and procedures that allowed it to get finished significantly faster than its competitors. You can imagine that, if Interiors gets a store done a week or two faster than anybody else, the store opens a week or two sooner, and that's a week or two of retail sales the store wouldn't otherwise have. That's real money, and money is always our metric of success.

The Aha Moment

As we were having the conversation about getting finished faster and all of the proof points around that (the techniques, processes, systems and procedures), the son of the owner said, "You know how on our signs at client sites, it says, 'Opening soon'? I want ours to say, 'Opening sooner.'" Everyone stopped and either said or thought, "That's brilliant!"

"Opening sooner" became this company's Core Proposition. In the moment it was blurted out, everybody *knew* it was right, and everybody *felt* it was right. Of course, we never just accept a Core Proposition without testing it. We shoot a lot of bullets at it to see whether the underlying logic can withstand the critical onslaught, as well as whether it works powerfully with all stakeholders. Let's look at Interiors' three main stakeholder groups to see if the Core Logic is relevant to them.

Customers. Since the Core Logic is usually uncovered in a conversation about customers, they are obviously relevant. What customer wouldn't want the shelving company to finish so quickly that it gets the option of opening sooner and generating revenue faster?

Employees. The Core Logic articulates what they already were doing, except it was going unrecognized. Articulating what they were doing, how they were doing it and the full value it delivers to the customer gives employees a sense of pride. It gives them a purpose that goes beyond just assembling retail shelving. And it now enables them to evangelize what they do in a concise, differentiated and passionate way.

Suppliers. If suppliers understand Interiors' mandate (opening sooner) and how they fulfill the mandate (the Core Logic), it gives them clear direction as to how to supply their products or services to Interiors in a more specific, customized way. This enables them to deliver greater value to Interiors and to the end client, and it gives them a sense of pride that they are making a bigger contribution.

The Core Logic of what Interiors does, the way it knits together its techniques, processes, systems and procedures, culminates in jobs getting finished faster. So the company was in the *category* of retail shelving, but in the *business* of opening sooner.

How Generic Self-Definitions Diminish Value

Another client of ours, Navigator, has an incredible reputation that was derived from doing two things extremely well: its work in political campaigns and in helping guide its clients, political or otherwise, out of crises. The reality is that while it does both of those things, it also does much more. What it doesn't do is traditional marketing strategy and communications. The company is filled with Type A personalities who thrive on dealing with the most intractable or threatening situations. They are adrenaline junkies.

Prior to its Blueprint, Navigator always described itself as a research-driven government relations and public relations company. This created two serious problems for the company:

1. When it would pitch a company that needed its services, it too often got turned down because the prospect already had market research, government relations or public relations suppliers.

2. When it did get retained, it was not able to charge fees that reflected the value it delivered. By associating itself with research, government relations and public relations companies, it trapped itself inside the accepted fee ranges of each of these disciplines. Even if it commanded the top end of those fee ranges, it didn't accurately reflect the value of what it accomplished for its clients. Because of the specialized work it did, and the magnitude of the problems it solved, Navigator should've been able to charge a much higher fee than any of these other kinds of companies. The cost to its client of not solving the problem is always massive.

This is the client we were telling you about previously, the one where one of the participants held out for almost two sessions, saying the Core Proposition that we were discussing at the time did not include his practice. He objected because his clients weren't in crisis; they felt *threatened*, but they weren't in crisis. In addition to that, this company's participation in political campaigns *did* fit the Core Proposition that was being contemplated, but only if you bent the definition of crisis a little bit to make it work. And finally, the company didn't see itself as just managing crises, even though that was the highest-profile part of its practice.

Your Core Proposition Is Rooted in Your Clients' Emotions

What we could all agree was the common thread tying all of Navigator's clients together was that they *felt* as if they were under some sort of threat, but not necessarily in a crisis. In the clients' minds, the consequences of these threats were far more grave than your garden-variety marketing or sales dilemma.

When we asked why the employees of this company were so good at what they do, we were told that they had all come from the world of politics, where both the mindset and skill set were clearly focused on winning. If you didn't win, you lost. There is no second place. There's first place and last place, and nothing in between. So when you're under threat, do you want to hire people who have marketing and communication skills to help you, or do you want a team of people who are absolutely tenacious when it comes to winning?

For most people, the answer would be obvious: they want the latter. But does that sound like a research-driven government relations and public relations company? When you hear what Navigator really does, and then compare it to how it articulates itself, there is a huge disconnect. There's a simple explanation for that: Navigator *isn't* a research-driven government and public relations company! It's a company that uses all of the tools of persuasion perfected in the battlefield of politics and applies them to situations in which its clients are under threat.

When we arrived at this realization, the CEO said, "All of these people feel like they can't afford to lose." We knew at the moment we heard this that he had just nailed Navigator's Core Proposition. If you're in a true crisis, you feel like you can't afford to lose. If you're running a political campaign and it's going well, you don't feel like you're in crisis, but you *do* feel as if you can't afford to lose. That's because the competition is so intense, and if you do lose, you are out of a job. And if the campaign is going badly, you definitely feel as though you are in a crisis you can't afford to lose. When our holdout heard "When you can't afford to lose," he said all of his clients feel that way, even though they might not be in crisis.

Everybody who knows the CEO, the company he founded and the people who work there say that is exactly what it does: it is in the business of "When you can't afford to lose."

What Do You Do?

A friend of ours at PricewaterhouseCoopers (PWC) introduced us to an interesting online publishing company, Elevate, that was started by a couple of really bright guys from Princeton University. It took about 45 minutes for them to do their pitch, and even then we were confused about what they did and why we would want to buy their service. But what little we could ascertain seemed intriguing and something that might be helpful to us.

After a long conversation about the company's story, the owners admitted that they were struggling with defining what they did, so it took a long time for prospective clients to understand it. Their story started with their time at Princeton, where there was a communication problem between research teams. They created an application that tried to solve that problem and, after many twists and turns along the way in what the application did, they arrived at where they were today, with a service for businesses that need to promote themselves more effectively. There was so much irrelevant detail in their story that people got lost in the minutiae and lost sight of the value of what they did. In other words, our reaction to their story was no different from anybody else's.

As we deconstructed the service, we realized that, in its simplest form, all it did was replicate something that practitioners in professional services firms have been doing for decades: seeing an article in a magazine that is relevant to a client, photocopying it, putting a sticky note on it with comments about why it is relevant, and sending it to the client. Their service gives you the ability to do this digitally, on a much larger scale and in a far more valuable way.

Here is how the service works for a tax lawyer in a law firm:

- Every morning, she receives an email with links to articles from the previous day on tax issues that are relevant to her clients.
- She skims through each of the articles and finds a few that she wants to send to her clients.
- For each of the articles that she is sending, she writes a brief note about why she thinks it is relevant to the client.
- The "send" button distributes the article to everyone on her designated mailing list, and out through her Twitter, LinkedIn and Facebook accounts.
- As a recipient of what she is publishing, if I am intrigued by one of her articles, I click on its link. This takes me to a web page with the article, as well as a header with her picture, her name, her contact information and her commentary on the article. That header stays in place the whole time I am reading the article. It is a great way of raising her profile and elevating her personal and corporate brand as an expert in that subject area.
- She then gets data showing her who opened the email, who clicked on what articles and who shared them through Facebook, LinkedIn and Twitter. This gives her valuable data on each member of her audience who engaged with her newsletter and how their reading interests identify them as a potential client for her services.

Our hypothetical tax lawyer is now publishing on a regular basis and, within her audience, becoming a subject-matter expert. The beauty of the Internet is that she can expand her audience without doing any work herself. People who read her emails and find the articles valuable may forward them automatically to their own audiences, each of whom now has the opportunity to subscribe to her email list. Or they can retweet her articles on Twitter or "like" them on Facebook with the click of a button, which creates the opportunity to spread her presence far and wide.

To truly understand the value of the service, we had to ask the question "Why do people in professional services firms send articles to their clients?" There were a number of answers that came to mind:

- As we mentioned above, to be perceived as a subject-matter expert.
- To make your clients feel as if you are always thinking about them.
- To strengthen your relationship with your clients, increasing their loyalty to you.

While all of these are true, none of them seems to be adequate to answer the question "Why should I choose you?" in a compelling enough way that we would say, "I want me some of that!" When we dug deeper, we got to the Core Logic underlying the value of the service.

Credibility Drives Sales

As a member of a professional services firm, one of the primary drivers of sales is your personal credibility and the credibility of your firm. One of the most successful ways to elevate your credibility is to publish—whether that be books, articles, op-ed pieces or blog posts. There are two broad kinds of content you can publish: content you write yourself and content others write.

The problem with writing content yourself is that many people can't write, and for those who can, they can't do it quickly.

Commenting on other people's content is a fast and more efficient way to publish, provided that the process of finding, commenting and publishing the content is quick and easy.

This company's service delivers relevant articles to you every day and gives you the ability to comment on and publish other people's content in just a few minutes. The result of using the service is that, over time, you elevate your credibility. Not surprisingly, then, the company's Core Proposition is "Elevate your credibility." For those in professional service firms, who wouldn't want that?

No doubt you have questions about the details of how the service works. But you get the gist of the service and its value to you from the previous paragraph. How long did it take you to read it? A minute or two? Contrast that with the 45 minutes it used to take the owners to tell their story.

Each of the three case studies above provides an example of the Core Logic of the business as it relates to the tangible need of the customer. It answers the question "What business are you really in?" Another way of expressing that is "What problem are you solving, and how?"

What we have yet to address is why the Core Proposition feels so right. Why it creates so a visceral a feeling in the customer that, when they hear it, it makes them say, "I want me some of that." We'll explain that in the next section: the complex world of Emotional Resonance.

Emotional Resonance
(How Does What You Do Affect Me Emotionally?)

In searching for a Core Proposition, it is critical to consider the emotional mindset of the customer.

As Simon Sinek points out in his book *Start with Why*, Apple is about changing the game in everything it does. Changing the game drives everything the company does and says, and it drives so many of us to line up for hours every time it introduces a new product. We don't line up to be the first to have its new products just because of their feature sets; we line up because of what using its products says about us to ourselves and to others. When we use its products, we believe *we* are game changers and we *feel* like we are game changers. We love how that makes us feel about ourselves and how it influences what others think of us. So your Core Proposition has a very important Emotional Resonance, which we will soon explain further.

Decisions Aren't Made Where You "Think"

The cerebral cortex is the part of the brain that processes facts, figures and rational thought. We think this is where we make decisions because this is where conscious thought—the little voices in our heads—resides. We know we are thinking, and thinking rationally, because we hear that little voice talking and rationalizing in our brains.

The limbic system is where we process feelings and emotions, and it is in the limbic system that we actually make our decisions. We think we're making our decisions rationally, but really we're making them based on how we feel—our emotions, our hunches and our intuitions. And then we use our cerebral cortex, the facts-and-figures part of our brain, to rationalize our decisions *after they are made*. It is because we make decisions in our limbic system that decisions *feel* right or *feel* like what we want.

A product's features and benefits are the facts and figures of the marketing world. We create and process features and benefits in our cerebral cortex, along with 90 per cent of the other rational arguments advertisers use in traditional marketing communications to try to persuade you to buy products and services. If you are talking to customers in the language of features and benefits alone, you are talking into the wrong part of their brains! You are talking into the cerebral cortex, which is not the part of the brain that makes decisions. It is like trying to convince somebody of something by speaking Italian when all they understand is English. You can talk compellingly in Italian until you are blue in the face, but they are never going to understand you.

To influence decision making, you need to speak into a person's limbic system. Your Core Proposition creates an Emotional Resonance because it speaks into your limbic system. If your "why" resonates with somebody emotionally, they will align with you. Your "why" is an expression of the cause you are committed to (in the case of Apple, "We change the game in everything we do"), not what you do or how you do it.

The president of a university was a new client of ours. As we were explaining the role of Emotional Resonance in a Blueprint to her, she told us that the limbic system was her area of academic specialty. She told us it was true that decision making happens in the limbic system and then jokingly added that she wished more decisions were made in the cerebral cortex on a rational basis, but unfortunately that wasn't the case.

What Emotional Resonance Looks Like

Let's start with the "Opening sooner" story we looked at earlier. If you are the VP at a big-box chain who is in charge of building a new store, the two things that are most important to you are being on time and on budget. Of all of the VP of construction's vast responsibilities, these are the two things that make him or her most stressed.

If our client does its job well, it means low stress for the VP while the construction job is in progress and when it gets finished on time. This is relatively simple and straightforward, and it is where the business thinking usually ends in trying to understand the relevance a company brings to its clients. Many companies would turn this into a marketing story about reducing the VP's stress by meeting the deadline.

But the VP is not just stressed about missing the deadline because of the deadline itself. He or she is accountable to others: superiors, peers, direct reports and suppliers. All of those people have decisions to make, and profit-and-loss, budget and timeline responsibilities to manage, that are dependent on the store opening on time. If the store opening has to be delayed, everyone in all the other departments of the company (and its suppliers) who are involved in the opening has to shift their schedules to accommodate the new deadline. This is hugely inconvenient for them and has the potential to make them angry with the VP of construction. His or her integrity, credibility and reputation are on the line. The threat to the VP due to a missed opening deadline causes fear, which in turn causes anxiety. The VP's emotional need is tied to the fear of all the personal and career consequences if the opening date is missed.

The Core Proposition "Opening sooner" speaks right into the fear that is always present in this VP's job, and that is why it has such strong Emotional Resonance. The emotion is fear, and the effect of the Core Proposition is to diminish that fear. Here's what "Opening sooner" says to the VP:

> *I'm not just promising to get you done on time. That is merely the cost of entry for my business. If I just promise to get you done on time, you'll still have the fear that I might not be finished on time right up until the deadline, and for that whole time you'll be feeling the stress that I'm causing because of the risk I might not make it. I am actually promising to get you done before the deadline so that you don't have to worry about the impact of what I'm doing on your deadline. Not only will I get it done before the deadline, I'll get it*

done well before the deadline so that you can actually become a hero
by starting to generate retail revenue faster.

When the Core Proposition is right, everything described in the previous paragraph flashes through the VP's mind just by hearing the words "Opening sooner." It's as if the Core Logic and its Emotional Resonance are lying dormant in the VP's brain, waiting to be awakened. The two words activate both the Core Logic and its Emotional Resonance, and when that happens, the VP intuitively and instantly makes logical connections that ultimately lead to the conclusion "Opening sooner = revenue sooner = I'm a hero." And that Emotional Resonance transforms fear into hope.

When the Core Proposition speaks into the Core Logic and its Emotional Resonance, the customer immediately *understands* and *feels* the value. And because the customer *feels* the value as well as understanding it, the Core Proposition speaks into the limbic system of the customer's brain, which is where the fear emotion lives and the decision-making happens.

Being Rational Doesn't Work!

Contrast this approach with what this company used to do, and what most companies do: trying to persuade their prospects to buy from them by using rational arguments. As an installer of retail shelving, it used to say things like "our customer service is better," "our people are nicer," "we have better communication with our clients" and (worst of all) "our price is lower." These are all banalities and genericisms that your client has heard a million times before from you and all of your competitors.

Now let's look at Navigator, the research-driven government and public relations company that discovered its Core Proposition is "When you can't afford to lose." The logical context for its clients is always the same: there is a serious threat that is causing, or could cause, a significant loss of money, reputation or status . . . or all of the above. Below are two examples, one that can be classified as a crisis threat and the other that could be classified as a threat, but not a crisis.

On the front page of the newspapers across the country the headline screamed, "Ex-politician kills bike courier." The news reports that followed described how the ex-politician was out "with a woman" when he got into a confrontation with a bike courier, whom he then drove into street furniture, mortally wounding him. The ex-politician drove to a nearby hotel and, according to the press, immediately phoned his lawyer and surrendered to the police. For the next few days, the ex-politician was vilified in the press, leaving his reputation destroyed and his current career as a senior public servant in tatters (he resigned shortly thereafter).

In fact, the call he made at the hotel was to our client, because the ex-politician knew he was in a crisis in which he couldn't afford to lose—he saw his whole future collapsing before his eyes. Within a few days, new details of the story started to emerge as a result of our client's research. The "woman" was his wife, and they were out to dinner for their wedding anniversary. Both of them are teetotallers, so alcohol was not a factor, as had been implied in some of the news stories. The bike courier had a history of mental illness, drug and alcohol abuse and violent behaviour—including earlier that day, when his ex-girlfriend was a victim of his anger and the police had to intervene. According to witnesses, because of the bike courier's uncontrollable anger, what had started as a minor incident quickly escalated into a situation where the courier had the ex-politician in a headlock while the ex-politician sat behind at the wheel of his car. Panicking, trying to get away to protect his wife and himself, and unable to see properly with his vision obscured by the headlock, the politician accidentally sideswiped some street furniture, the impact of which killed the courier.

None of the courier's sad and troubled history justifies what happened to him, but knowing that new information certainly gives you a different perspective on the ex-politician's actions, a perspective that is more sympathetic and understanding. This was the beginning of how our client helped the ex-politician by presenting a more balanced appreciation of the situation.

The ex-politician was in a situation that he had never experienced before, that he never in a million years imagined he would be in and that he was totally out of his depth in handling on his own. He needed the help of people who had been through these kinds of crisis situations before and knew what actions needed to be taken to deal with it properly.

The emotional context here is defined by fear and possibly even panic. We can only imagine the fear that was racing through the ex-politician's brain that night and in the following days because of the death he had caused the courier and how his own life had been destroyed as a result. The impact of this unfortunate event would ripple through his immediate family (his wife and children), his extended family, his friends and acquaintances, and his peers in politics and business—not to mention the family and friends of the courier.

As he was struggling with this extreme emotional turmoil, you can imagine that if he heard the phrase "When you can't afford to lose," he would've said to himself, "Oh my God, that is *exactly* how I feel . . . you understand me. Can you can help me?" To which our client would reply, "We're on your side, we are here to help and there is hope." You wouldn't be surprised, in this fictional conversation, if the ex-politician would be so relieved that he would actually burst out in tears. A Core Proposition like "When you can't afford to lose" has a powerful emotional impact in a situation like this and in almost any other crisis.

The second case study for this company is an example that is a threat but not a crisis (a crisis is a particular kind of threat, but there are other kinds of threats as well). An industry group had a monopoly over the management of its particular jurisdiction. Its practitioners require an unbelievable amount of training and experience, and the consequences of failure in their work can be catastrophic. Government regulators were considering allowing a related industry group, one whose practitioners have a fraction of the training, to take over many of these responsibilities because this arrangement would be more cost-effective.

In the minds of the members of the original industry group, this legislation would be disastrous to both themselves and their customers. Logically, they believed that they couldn't afford to lose this battle because they would suffer the loss of their livelihood and, in their view, client safety would be severely compromised.

The Emotional Resonance is rooted in the many impacts of the loss of livelihood and professional status. They felt the public would be put at risk. An affluent lifestyle would be threatened, as would the practitioners' ability to provide for their families and the social and economic levels to which they have become accustomed. Their sense of self-worth is determined in part by their ability to provide for their families. Also threatened was their social status, which is also a contributor to their self-worth. And finally, there is the sheer sense of personal helplessness that they felt when they foresaw that their livelihood was to be taken from them. The proposed legislation wasn't just a threat to their industry, it was a personal attack on the self-worth of each and every one of the practitioners. When such deep and important feelings are at stake, the expression "When you can't afford to lose" has a powerful emotional impact.

Now let's look at the Emotional Resonance of the online publishing company's service. The Core Logic is based on the idea that if you publish consistently on your particular topic of specialization, you will become a subject-matter expert. This will elevate your credibility in a business where the credibility of you and your firm is a primary sales driver.

A hypothetical tax lawyer is a member of a 600-lawyer firm, but, because of the way law firms are structured, she is really one of 600 individual businesses all sharing the same office and the same company name. Her salary, bonus and promotions are all based on her billing rate and the hours she bills to the clients she brings into the firm. It is a classic example of eating what you kill—and if you don't kill, you starve. When the phone is constantly ringing with new business, this isn't an issue. But when it isn't . . .

There is always a lingering fear in our tax lawyer's mind that it could all disappear tomorrow. And if it does, she will feel like a failure, professionally and personally. In a worst-case scenario, she will lose her job and be disgraced as a lawyer . . . or at least that's how she *feels*. If she has a family, she will *feel* as if she is inadequate as a provider and as a mother. Billings, or lack thereof, have a huge emotional impact on her emotional well-being. And at the root of that impact is fear. Remember, this doubt, this lingering fear, could be operating even if her business is going gangbusters because of the apprehension, real or imagined, that it could all disappear tomorrow.

A flip side of fear is hope. If you buy the logic of this company's service, you will feel hope. You recognize that your credibility and that of your firm do drive sales. This service gives you a powerful ability to, at minimum, elevate your own credibility. You have a greater sense of control over the success of your future because you have a means that is totally within your control to drive sales by elevating your credibility, and that gives you hope.

There is another emotional operative at play here, and that is ego. Publishing puts you on a public stage. While some people shy away from the limelight—it truly scares them—many people like the attention, even if they won't admit it. The act of publishing constantly helps you create a public profile that constantly feeds your ego. And if you are getting positive feedback on the quality of what you're publishing, that feeds your ego even more. When you hear the Core Proposition "Elevate your credibility" and the explanation of how the service does that for you, you immediately make the connection to ego gratification, even if it's only on a sub-conscious level.

In summary, the Emotional Resonance this company's service has on customers is mitigating fear/creating hope and feeding your ego.

What a Core Proposition Is and What It Isn't

At the top of this chapter, we used a DNA metaphor to describe your Core Proposition. Like DNA, it defines the organization at the deepest emotional level. But for what? The purpose of your Core Proposition is to give the organization a total focus on the one thing that makes it uniquely remarkable. The reason why you have to dive so deep to identify your Core Proposition, as opposed to what you have to do to develop a tagline or a positioning statement, is because it has to endure for the next 15 or 20 years.

We know that sounds a little strange—who in business has the luxury of looking ahead that far? The answer is that a company is what it is, and it will always be that way deep down. It may change the strategies and tactics it uses to be who it is—in the same way that people upgrade their education, undergo therapy or use other means to change the direction of their lives. But they don't become different people. They become modified versions of who they are, but who they are never goes away.

When your Core Proposition is right, it keeps you on a very singular path while at the same time allowing you a wide range of ways to stay on that path. Looking at our shelving company example, over time other companies will copy what they do. So what do they do to stay ahead? This is a tough question for most companies because they have the capability to go in so many directions. For our shelving company, its Core Proposition tells it to go in only one direction: more "Opening sooner." To innovate and stay ahead, the business must figure out more ways to open sooner, because as long as stores are being built or renovated, the benefits of opening sooner will be powerful and/or valuable. There is an infinite number of ways to open sooner that have yet to be discovered.

A Core Proposition is not a positioning statement or a slogan. This may seem a little confusing, since all three examples we have given you (Opening sooner, When you can't afford to lose, Elevate your credibility) sound like slogans. In fact, about a third of our clients are able to use their Core Propositions as slogans because they have great marketing and sales appeal. But fully two-thirds of our clients have Core Propositions that do a great job of guiding everything the company does and says but really can't be expressed publicly. The value of the Core Proposition is enduring, while the value of a positioning statement or a slogan will last only as long as it is relevant to current market conditions and customer needs or demands.

We want to make one final comment on a Core Proposition versus a positioning statement and the tagline. When you know your Core Proposition, you then develop a positioning statement from it and a slogan from your positioning statement. The positioning statement has to consider a number of things: it has to be true to the Core Proposition; it has to take into account current market conditions, including what your competitors are doing; and it has to factor in the needs and wants of customers at that point in time. The market conditions, the competitive situation and the needs and wants of customers are all variables that will change over time. So both the positioning statement and the tagline you adopt will likely also change over time. What won't change over time is your Core Proposition.

Both "Opening sooner" and "When you can't afford to lose" were used as slogans. There may come a time when the respective companies change their slogans to something else. They will do that because something in the marketplace has changed and a different positioning statement or slogan will do a better job of generating sales. But even if their positioning statements and slogans change multiple times over the years, the shelving company will still be about "Opening sooner" and the company that helps you deal with threats to your business or to you personally will still be in the business of "When you can't afford to lose."

The Relationship Between the Core Proposition and Its Core Logic

Once you have discovered the Core Logic of your business, determined its emotional impact and revealed your Core Proposition in the course of those conversations, the question becomes "How do they all fit together?" The relationship among the three works like this:

- The Core Proposition is the expression—in seven words or less—of the Core Logic.
- Saying the Core Proposition to someone triggers an intuitive understanding of the Core Logic, even though the person couldn't necessarily articulate the Core Logic.
- The intuitive understanding of the Core Logic is rooted in its emotional impact.
- The intuitive understanding of the Core Logic and its emotional impact makes the person say, "I want me some of that!"

It is the way these three elements work together that causes the depth of both understanding and feeling about your business in the people who are most important to you: your customers, prospects, employees, investors, board members, strategic partners and all other stakeholders.

Say the Core Proposition → *Understand the Core Logic* → *Feel the Emotional Impact*

So now that we know what a Core Proposition is and isn't, let's look at how you use it to guide everything your organization does and says. In the next chapter, we will look at how you use your Core Proposition to shape the parts of the company, the way it operates, the way it is structured, and your products and services in order to be more competitive. And in the chapter following that one, we'll show you how to use a Core Proposition to guide everything your organization says, both internally to your employees and externally to all your stakeholders, not the least of whom are your customers.

4

Cutting to the Core

In Seven Words or Less

United Van Lines' Core Proposition

A moving company came to us with an interesting conundrum: it felt there was a disconnect between head office and the member companies that was both frustrating and inhibiting the growth of the company. One of the mandates of head office was to come up with new operations, marketing ideas and sales initiatives that they would either offer to, or execute on behalf of, the member companies. The problem was that the member companies weren't using some of the initiatives and, as a result, were not seeing the value of what head office was doing for them.

For instance, head office negotiated a pennies-per-gallon discount for its members' trucks from a national gas retailer. The potential savings on an annual basis was substantial, but a lot of members weren't taking advantage of this program. When head office dug into the reasons why, it found that many members were too far away from the gas retailer's locations to make the program worthwhile.

What made this problem even more acute is the fact that this organization is a reverse franchise. The franchisees—the members—banded together to create the head office, not the other way around as with a traditional franchise organization. So when head office talks about serving "customers," its customers are the member companies, not the people who are moving from one house to another. Head office, which brought us into the organization, was very concerned that it was not serving its customers/members as effectively as it could.

As the Blueprint progressed, head office kept asking us whether the Core Proposition that emerged would be relevant to its customers' customers as well (the people moving to a new home). In other words, would the Core Proposition resonate with the member moving companies *and* with consumers who are hiring the company to move their belongings from one house to another? At the end of the day, the Core Proposition has to resonate with all stakeholder groups, so you can focus on one to get the answer for everyone. Usually, focusing on the customer is the best route to the Core Proposition. United Van Lines was skeptical but gave us the benefit of the doubt.

We examined many service scenarios customers encounter with a moving company, as well as those that moving companies had with head office. The one that proved most insightful involved people moving from one house to another. They typically have one of two experiences: they're very happy because the moving truck arrived on time and nothing was broken, or they're very unhappy because the moving truck was late and some of their belongings were broken.

If you are part of a family that is moving and you're waiting at your new house for the moving truck, the two things that are likely to cause the most stress are wondering whether the truck will arrive on time and whether any of your belongings will be damaged or broken. The on-time issue is important because it speaks to people's sense of control. Most people don't need to be *controlling* per se, but they do want a sense of control over what is happening in their lives. At the time of the Blueprint, the way most moving companies worked was that the truck showed up when it showed up. If it was going to be late, even if it was usually for a totally legitimate and unavoidable reason (for instance, traffic jams due to car accidents), the customer was often left in the dark.

Now imagine standing there on your new front lawn, looking up and down the street, waiting for the big truck with all of your possessions. Or worse, you are moving into an apartment or condo and have a specific time scheduled for the service elevator. If the truck is late—even just one minute late—the doubts begin to creep into your mind. You have no idea whether the truck is coming around the corner momentarily or tomorrow. The uncertainty is a direct assault on your sense of control and causes, at minimum, stress. The more time passes, the more you curse the moving company. In that moment, it is very hard for you to imagine that the truck driver has been stuck for hours on the highway because of an accident and is feeling incredible stress because an angry customer awaits.

As you stand fuming on the lawn, you conclude that this company just doesn't care about you. If you knew the real circumstances, you would know nothing is further from the truth. But you don't know those circumstances. You are in the dark. So, when the truck shows up a couple of hours late, it is met by a hostile customer who vows never to use the driver's company again. Meanwhile, the driver who was making every effort but was trapped by unavoidable circumstances is left feeling that the customer is being unreasonable.

Contrast this with the scenario in which the truck shows up on time or earlier and none of the customer's possessions are broken. The reality is that the customer was likely feeling anxiety right up until the truck arrived from worry that it might be late and that things might be broken. When the truck is on time and everything is intact, the customer feels a tremendous sense of relief, possibly even elation. What the customer is left with is a wonderful experience that, hopefully, the person will feed back to the company and his or her friends. This satisfaction might not be expressed in these specific words, but the customer would say something that implied the company cared.

Now think back to the example of the fuel discount program that head office devised and negotiated for the benefit of its member companies. Head office was quite proud of this accomplishment because it should save each truck thousands of dollars every year. But the response from many of the member companies was one of disinterest because they couldn't take advantage of the program. These member companies concluded that head office just didn't care about them.

The underlying factor in each of these situations is the *perceived* standard of care. So whether we are talking about head office and a member company or a member company and its customers, the standard of care is everything. It is the primary driver, pardon the pun, of the relationship. If the perceived standard of care is high, the relationship is strong. If it is low, the relationship is weak. So the Core Proposition for this moving company is "A higher standard of care."

"A higher standard of care" may seem like a cliché that could apply to any and every company. On the surface this is true, but it works in this specific situation because we are looking for a phrase that addresses the emotional impact of a perceived lack of service to both customers and member companies. Remember, we aren't looking for a slogan, we're looking for an internal strategic expression that resonates when customers and member companies are dissatisfied because they don't perceive head office cares about them. Constantly striving for and achieving "A higher standard of care" will mitigate the frustration that customers and member companies feel. What we hope to show you in subsequent chapters is how "A higher standard of care" provides clear and tangible guidance to the company about how it delivers its services to customers and member companies. So the fact that it is a cliché doesn't matter. It does its job.

Baycrest Hospital's Core Proposition

Baycrest started as a long-term care (LTC) facility for the Jewish community in Toronto. It was very well supported by the Jewish community since its creation over 90 years ago and had become the gold standard in LTC. It started doing research, and over time became one of the top five facilities in the world for research into the aging brain. Baycrest was embarking on its largest fund-raising campaign ever and, after a number of unsuccessful attempts to do so, hired us to help define what it was going to be in the future.

As the CEOs of both the hospital and its foundation explained to us, Baycrest can't call itself a care facility because that will alienate all the people who work for and donate to the research side. It can't call itself a research facility because, in turn, that would alienate all the people who work for and donate to the hospital. It was made clear to us that unifying both parts of Baycrest under a single banner that made everybody comfortable had to be the objective of this exercise.

As we were driving to Baycrest for a Blueprint session, we started discussing the Centers for Disease Control and Prevention (CDC) in Atlanta. We wanted to know why, in naming the organization, they pluralized the word *centers*. A layperson would see the CDC as just one organization with many departments. But we realized that each of these departments specialized in something that, in the view of everybody related to any particular department, was entirely different from any of the other departments. Each department would consider itself to be an island unto itself. Pluralizing *centers* recognized each department as a unique entity while at the same time making it a part of a larger whole.

It occurred to us that this applied to Baycrest as well. While the research department knew it was part of Baycrest, it thought of itself as entirely different from the care side. And the reverse was true for the hospital. So the idea of "centres" seems to apply to Baycrest very well.

Then we started talking about the fact that the LTC hospital was the gold standard for the region. You don't achieve this recognition just by treating your patients well. You have to develop new and better ways to treat and take care of elderly people. In other words, you have to innovate to be the leader. Research, by its very nature, is innovation. So both sides of Baycrest were committed to innovation in aging.

When we put together the two notions—"centres" and "innovation in aging"—we came up with a new name for the facility: the Baycrest Centres for Innovation in Aging. When we presented it to the Blueprint team at the start of that session, they immediately fell in love with it. They spent about half an hour waxing on about the importance of pluralizing the word *centres* for the very reason we explained above . . . and for the naming-rights opportunities this created for the foundation. Then they spent a long time talking about how accurately "Innovation in aging" captured all aspects of what Baycrest did. The hospital's CEO even went so far as to say, "That's why I was put on this planet. To do innovation in aging."

As well, what we all realized is that Baycrest's Core Proposition was contained inside its proposed name: Innovation in aging. We then looked at a number of areas of the hospital and the research facility and discussed how they had to be transformed in the future in order to be true to the Core Proposition (see chapter 10).

Deluxe Toronto's Core Proposition

Deluxe Toronto is known as a leader in postproduction servicing in Canada and is a component of Deluxe Toronto Entertainment Services Group. Unfortunately, classifying Deluxe Toronto as postproduction excludes many of the "newer world" services that it provides in the field of film and television production.

Deluxe Toronto still does postproduction, but the list of other services it provides to its clients is extensive:

Duplication
Watermarking
Conversions
Encoding
Digital storage
Digital distribution
Closed-captioning
Web watch

Don't worry if you don't know what any of these things are; suffice it to say they aren't postproduction. The reason Deluxe Toronto's service offering is expanding out of its traditional area is because technology and competition are shrinking the market for traditional postproduction. Deluxe Toronto has been very successful in evolving to meet the new realities of its market.

When it was just a postproduction company, it could tell people in the business what it was, but it struggled with explaining why it was better. Now that it has expanded beyond postproduction, it can't even tell people what it is anymore. That was the challenge going into Blueprint: Who are you and how do you do better?

To determine what Deluxe Toronto had become, you have to understand the nature of film and television production. To the layperson, it can seem like the director is the person in charge, but

in fact it's the producer. The producer has the ultimate accountability for getting the project finished—financially and logistically.
If you have ever been on the set of a movie or TV shoot, it seems
like chaos. Everybody and nobody seems to be in charge. There's a
lot of walking around and doing stuff without any apparent rhyme
or reason. A very, very small percentage of time is spent actually
shooting. If you are unfamiliar with the business, you wonder how
they get anything done.

In fact, the production of a major movie or television show is
one of the most highly organized organisms you will ever encounter.
The people managing the production, with the producer at the top,
have exceptional organizational skills and ability to handle unbelievable stress. The production of the film is a classic example of "the
best-laid plans of mice and men," so the key decision makers are
constantly having to adapt and improvise as the shoot progresses.

Another characteristic of TV and film production is that
many, if not most, of the people working in it are subcontract-
ors. They aren't employees; they're suppliers to whoever owns the
rights to the movie. It would be difficult enough if the producer
had to manage that many employees. But the producer is actually
managing many, many suppliers and, directly and indirectly, all
of *their* suppliers and employees. With all that is going on, and all
that can go wrong, and all the money at stake, it is a wonder that
anybody would want the job of a film producer.

This is the world in which Deluxe Toronto thrives, originally
as a subcontractor to do postproduction and now as a subcontractor to do so much more. Here's the logic of the value of the
services it provides. Imagine a rickety old train from the 1800s,
barrelling down the track at a rapid rate of speed. There are people
hanging on for dear life on the roof and others sticking out the
windows. As the train rocks back and forth, people fall off, only
to be grabbed by somebody on the train and pulled safely back on

board in the nick of time before they hit the ground. Somehow, the train reaches its destination safely, and all of the passengers dust themselves off and disembark.

This is the metaphor that represents the making of a feature film. The director is the engineer driving the train, and he or she has the responsibility of keeping it on the track. The producer not only supervises the director but is in charge of everything else on the train, including the health and welfare of the passengers and what every employee is doing to make their trip as safe and enjoyable as possible. There can be no question that the director's job is difficult, but the producer's is near impossible.

Now imagine somebody who's always by the producer's side, and every time there is a complication, that person tells the producer, "Let me take care of that for you." Assuming that person does a great job, the producer will come to view him or her as invaluable. In the real world, every time Deluxe Toronto says, "Let me take care of that for you," it is creating a new product or service that is really helpful to the producer.

This is the genius of Deluxe Toronto's successful adaptation to the new world of film production. There are so many things that can go wrong. In essence, every time Deluxe Toronto looks for one of those things that can go wrong and creates a solution for it, it is telling the producer, "Let me show you an easier way to do that." Every time it develops a new product or service, it is solving a problem for the producer and making his or her life a little easier. On top of that, each of those problems adds a little or a lot of stress to the producer's life. In a producer's eyes, anyone who can reduce his or her stress is a godsend.

Deluxe Toronto's Core Proposition is "An easier way." It looks at the world through the producer's eyes and finds ways large and small to make the producer's job easier. Every time it does, it turns that into a new product or service. As one example, there are many people who need to see an advance copy of a film. Film critics need to see an advance copy so they can write their reviews and have them published on the same day the film is released. Since advance copies are distributed digitally, there is a very high risk that they will end up on the web, free for anyone to download. Deluxe Toronto created a service that custom-watermarks every single advance copy. Each person who receives an advance copy gets their own unique watermark. If an advance copy of the movie ends up on the web, Deluxe Toronto can see whose watermark is on it and inform the producers of the film so that they can take appropriate action against that specific person.

Bloom Burton & Co.'s Core Proposition

Bloom Burton, one of Canada's leading health care investment firms, provides a wide variety of services to health care and biotech companies. These companies are either start-ups or at the early to middle stages of product development. They are typically relatively small and totally focused on their products or their area of expertise.

Two factors that these companies have in common are that they need capital to fuel their innovations and they are hoping for a big payday down the road. In order to get the investment they require and achieve the exit they dream about, they have to present themselves to the financial community in a way that maximizes their value. But this is not a skill set that these companies usually have internally; they must either try their best to do it themselves, even though they don't have the expertise (not recommended!), or have to hire experts to guide them through the process. This is where Bloom Burton comes in.

While Bloom Burton was capable of helping its clients in all areas of financing, from investment to exit, it couldn't tell its story in a way that let prospects see the full breadth of their offering. Its sales process involved listening to the prospect and then pitching whichever of its many services it sounded like the prospect needed the most. It would then try to explain that it had a variety of other services that would also be beneficial to the prospect. This presented two problems: Too often, the prospect would narrowly perceive Bloom Burton as specializing in whatever service it pitched first. Or the prospect would be confused by what seemed like a disjointed collection of services.

The latter problem arose because Bloom Burton was actually three entities. Bloom Burton itself helped companies through private and public financings, mergers and acquisitions, and research. Vancia Group provided management consulting services. It also ran an investment fund that would invest directly in companies with promising products. This fragmentation of brands and services resulted in a confusing story.

What Bloom Burton didn't realize was that it actually did only one thing, and each of these components contributed to that one thing. If it could determine the one thing it did and support that with its portfolio of services, prospects in the health care community at large would have a much clearer understanding of what Bloom Burton had to offer. But what was that one thing?

In trying to uncover Bloom Burton's Core Proposition, we realized that all of the principals and investors in all prospect companies want the same thing, which is a monetizing event. A monetizing event could be investment, a loan, a merger or acquisition, being acquired, an IPO or a successful introduction of its product to market. These are the kinds of paydays that entrepreneurs dream about. Navigating the byzantine world of finance towards one of these monetizing events can be arduous and heartbreaking if it is unsuccessful, or arduous and exhilarating if successful. Whatever the outcome, the path to money is difficult at best.

How difficult it is to navigate that path depends on two things: the quality of the company's product and how effectively the company and its story are packaged to the financial community. The latter process is very complex. This is where Bloom Burton comes in. Each of its services addresses a different aspect of packaging a company. The more effectively and comprehensively a company is packaged, the greater the likelihood it will achieve its monetizing event. With a monetizing event as the ultimate goal, the logic of Bloom Burton's services is simple: with them, the company will have a faster path to monetization. This is how Bloom Burton's Core Proposition became "A faster path to monetization."

"Our Core Proposition was the common thread that tied all of our services together," says Brian Bloom, co-founder and president of Bloom Burton. "It was the higher purpose that we were working towards on behalf of our clients. We were no longer a disjointed collection of companies, brands and services. 'A faster path to monetization' defined who we were, and our services became the means to get there.

"When we discovered that our Core Proposition was 'A faster path to monetization,' it triggered a profound aha moment for us," says Bloom. "In that moment, we switched from being a company selling services that *some* companies wanted to a company selling an outcome that *everybody* wanted. I can't overstate how important this transformation was for us. It completely changed our perspective on our business. In a moment, it was as if we were reborn as a new, more powerful company."

VHA Home HealthCare's Core Proposition
VHA Home HealthCare is a 90-year-old not-for-profit organization that provides home health care services to those who are recuperating at home and the elderly who need help at home. It helps people remain in the community, instead of in a hospital or long-term care facility, for as long as possible. It relies on government contracts, donations and fees to provide its services. VHA

competes against other not-for-profit organizations and for-profit organizations, and with the combination of increasing competition and shrinking government resources, it needed to create a sustainability plan for its business model.

The challenge in VHA's Blueprint was to define and articulate its core differentiation, to make sure that everything it did was aligned with who it is at its core and to tell a more compelling story so that it could compete more effectively. The conversation that drove VHA's Blueprint was around the vulnerability and dependency of its clients—the patients and seniors who were in their homes. Two factors drove this conversation:

1. The longer clients stay vulnerable and dependent, the more expensive they are for the health care system. The sooner they become independent, or at least more independent, the less it costs the government to support them.
2. Being admitted into a medical facility robs these people of their independence and quality of life. Also, there is lots of research that shows that people who are sick or injured recuperate faster at home than they do in the hospital.

While VHA provided a variety of services for its clients, the conversation revealed that the end goal was always the same: greater independence. When we realized that fact, it became obvious to all of us that VHA's Core Proposition was "More independence." In other words, VHA was in the business of creating more independence for its clients. The inclusion of the word *more* is important, because independence is not always possible. In the case of the senior who is able to live at home but not fully able to look after herself, full independence is not a likely outcome. But the more independent this senior can remain, the less costly it will be for the health care system to support her.

Longo's Core Proposition

Longo's is a classic story of a successful multigenerational family business. Started in 1956 by Tommy, Joe and Gus Longo, it has grown to become one of the most successful supermarket chains in Canada. Despite its success, it is a David among Goliaths in the supermarket industry and is constantly threatened by the size of its bigger competitors.

The larger chains have more leverage with—and get better pricing from—suppliers because of the volume of products they buy from them. They also have much larger marketing budgets than Longo's, which gives them a distinct advantage in an advertising-driven business. In spite of this, Longo's has managed to survive and thrive because of the unique way it runs its business.

At the heart of what makes it special isn't just its products, produce or service, but an ethos that runs through every aspect of the business. There is a common thread to how the company is structured, how it manages its people, how it selects products, how it works with suppliers and, most important, how it treats its customers. Longo's knew intuitively that it did things differently, but as supermarket competition heated up and the pressure to reduce prices mounted, it knew it had to capture and articulate how it did things differently in order to expand its business less by intuition and more by design.

It became apparent in the conversation during Longo's Blueprint that the glue that bound the family together into a tight-knit unit for all these decades also bound every aspect of the business together. It was that glue—the Longo family values—that we had to articulate in seven words or less. That is how "Treating you like family" became Longo's Core Proposition. The Longo family treated each other like family at home and treated everybody related to their business like family at work. That ethos impacted every aspect of their business, from how they hired, trained and rewarded their staff, to how they bought and presented produce in the store, to how they selected the other products they sold and how they related to the broader customer community.

"Selling food in a supermarket is generic unless you are guided by something bigger," says Anthony Longo. "It is so easy to slip into business speak, but our Core Proposition always regrounds us in what matters to our customers and employees." "Treating you like family" is now the mantra that drives everything the company does and says.

Eckler's Core Proposition

The senior partners at Eckler had each been in the business of defined-benefit pensions for decades. As experienced practitioners, they were supremely confident in their ability to deliver value to their clients.

"When we were solely in the business of consulting to defined-benefit pension plans, we knew we could deliver," says Jill Wagman, Eckler's managing principal. "But we knew that defining ourselves narrowly as being in the business of defined-benefit pension consulting was too limiting, and a path to a difficult future. We had to figure out where we were going to get sales from next, but we didn't know what else we could do. We were frustrated because we felt constrained by our own self-definition."

Eckler no longer defines the business it is in as defined-benefit pension consulting. It is in the business of "A greater degree of certainty." When you define yourself this way, the world opens up to you. To find new business, all you have to do is look for companies that are experiencing uncertainty and determine whether they have sufficient data that could be used to build Eckler's predictive actuarial models. These companies become qualified prospects for a company that specializes in "A greater degree of certainty."

"We now have business opportunities in areas of business we never expected, projects that have nothing to do with defined-benefit pensions," says Wagman. "We never would have considered pitching for this kind of business in the past because we would have felt like pretenders based on our prior self-definition of being specialists in defined-benefit pensions. Realizing that we're actually in the business of creating a greater degree of certainty for our clients, for us and for our stakeholders, changed us. Without actually doing anything differently, we realized that with our actuarial modelling and data management skills, we had far more capability and that there was all of this business out there outside of the defined-benefit pensions realm that was available to us. Our new definition of the business we were in gave us the confidence to go out and pitch this business and really think and *feel* like we were experts who could deliver better value than anyone else."

Momentum's Core Proposition

"We knew we had a good idea with a unique business model, but we had so much trouble articulating it in a way that people could see its value. This really inhibited our ability to get the funding that was required to get our first development off the ground," says Drew McDougall, the founder and CEO of a start-up called Momentum.

Momentum builds condos that are targeted towards people downsizing out of their traditional family homes because their children have moved away. In the past, these people would be approaching their retirement. They would be at or near age 65 and would be looking forward to not having to work anymore. The problem is, people don't think of themselves in those terms anymore. Retirement isn't for people in their 50s, 60s or even 70s. They are just entering a new phase in their lives and will be working full time, part time or not at all. Even if they are going to spend this time travelling or doing leisure activities, they don't see themselves as retired because that's for people much older than them.

So the traditional definition of retiree doesn't work as a way to classify potential customers. If you called them retirees, they would immediately rule themselves out because they don't see themselves as being a part of that group.

One of the challenges of the Blueprint was figuring out how to characterize the target group. Potential buyers had reached the stage in their life when their children had all moved away from home, they were rattling around in a house that was too big for them and they were looking for something smaller. They didn't want to deal with the cost and effort of maintaining a residence that was too big for them.

We realized that we couldn't characterize these people by age. What we did instead was to characterize them by situation. What was the major life shift that they were contemplating in that moment? They were downsizing—therefore, they are *downsizers*. The beauty of this characterization is that there is no negative age implication to it as there is with *retiree*. If you are at that phase in your life where you are selling your home to buy a condo, you are downsizing. If somebody calls you a downsizer, you would say, "Yes, of course I am." It is what you are doing and who you are, and there is no negative baggage associated with that term.

A search of the web showed us that, while we didn't invent this term, it was very uncommon. It was an obscure term mostly used to describe the process of stripping away the excess from your life in order to lead a more sustainable lifestyle. Since it wasn't used at all in the residential development world, it was a term we could define for our target group, popularize in the condo world and own.

Momentum's condo model, in itself, is not a novel idea. What is unique to Momentum's developments is that the base of each building, called the podium, will be filled with retailers and services that are essential to people who have reached this stage in their lives. For instance, since these people are either approaching or in retirement, they have a heightened sense of their own health, well-being and mortality. Every one of the Momentum developments will have a medical clinic that will serve not only the condo, but the surrounding community as well.

If you were to describe McDougall's business in the traditional way, it would seem obvious that he is a condo developer. But that doesn't capture his unique business model of filling the podium with services and retailers that meet the most essential needs of his buildings' residents. Therefore, McDougall describes himself (his Core Proposition) as being in the business of "catering to downsizers' most essential needs."

Emeritus Financial Strategies' Core Proposition

The challenge in the wealth management field is that most firms and financial advisors don't have a compelling reason to choose them. The standard pitch is that they come to understand your unique financial needs both now and in the future, they customize a solution for you and then they implement that solution. This is not only the typical procedure in the wealth management field, it is also the general process followed by all service-industry firms, whether they are in finance or not. Advertising agencies, lawyers, technology suppliers and accountants, to name a few, all follow that same process.

Doug Dahmer, the founder of Emeritus Financial, a wealth management firm, was frustrated with his inability to quickly and easily explain his unique methodology for financial management. It is not only a complex methodology, it goes against the accepted wisdom in the financial services industry. "The world is essentially divided into two kinds of investing," says Dahmer. "Those who buy and hold and those who try to time the market. Those who advocate for buy and hold believe this is a universal panacea for low-risk investing and guaranteed returns. It is based on the logic

83

that the stock market is constantly rising over long periods of time, even though it bounces up and down when looked at over short periods."

The challenge with this thinking, according to Dahmer, is that historically there are two kinds of market cycles, each of which runs for approximately 20 years. One cycle, as we experienced from approximately 1980 to 2000, is a constantly increasing market. The buy-and-hold strategy works in this market cycle because, even though there will be ups and downs, the overall value of stocks rises over that time span. The second kind of market cycle shows almost no growth or even a decline over a two-decade period. If you invest $100 at the beginning of this kind of cycle, you will have approximately $100 at its end. "You need a different kind of approach during the flat market cycle, because obviously buy and hold doesn't work here," says Dahmer.

Dahmer used to work for big wealth management firms but got frustrated that they were selling buy-and-hold products, such as mutual funds, to their clients during flat market cycles. "This is not in the client's best interest because at best they will make modest gains over a long period of time, and at worst they will lose money," says Dahmer. "But it is in the best interest of the financial services firms to recommend mutual funds because they make a substantial profit from them and they are so easy to sell. It is easy to convince clients that the accepted wisdom of buy-and-hold investing is the right choice, even though it doesn't serve them in a flat market cycle." Dahmer started Emeritus with the belief that you have to treat the two market cycles very differently.

Another aspect of Dahmer's methodology is different. "What the average investor doesn't realize is that whatever gains you make as you are investing your money can be wiped out by a poor strategy for drawing it down once you retire," says Dahmer. "Your drawdown strategy is almost more important than your investing strategy because it has such a huge impact on how much money you keep and how much you lose to taxes once you retire. Most financial advisors don't have the tax understanding to appreciate how much can be lost during the drawdown phase, so they have no plan for how to do that effectively."

Although we had worked with a number of wealth management firms, we had never heard this story before. It was a bit of an eye-opener for us. Dahmer explained to us that there is a class of investor that understands the two different market cycles and the importance of understanding how you will draw down the money when you need it as you get older: those who are rich enough to have their own private stable of money managers. Dahmer calls these people "the smart money" because they tailor their investing strategies to whatever long-term cycle we are in and they have clearly thought through a detailed plan for drawing down that money in a way that maximizes their tax savings.

When we first heard Dahmer use the term *the smart money,* it reverberated in our heads. Our immediate reaction was that *we* want to do what the smart money does. It made us feel like we were missing something, like we were at a disadvantage, if we didn't do what the smart money does. Who wouldn't want the investing advantages of the superrich? The more we talked about what the smart money does, the more we realized that Dahmer is a human divining rod for smart-money investing strategies. Whatever the smart money does, Dahmer follows. That is how we landed on the Core Proposition "Following the smart money" for Emeritus.

"I had struggled with articulating the complexity of my approach for years," says Dahmer. "But 'Following the smart money' summed it up in four words that made people want that as soon as they heard it. Once people hear that this is how the smart money invests and draws down their wealth as they need it, they understand the details of how it is done much more quickly and completely. Where their eyes used to glaze over, they are now fully engaged in the conversation because they want the advantages of the smart money so badly!"

IQMH's Core Proposition

Whenever a doctor has a question about a patient's health, the first step is almost always to get lab tests done. Once the lab tests return, the doctor has insight into the patient's health and a course of action is taken. When you think of the magnitude of the health care system—all the doctors, hospitals, clinics, medical technology, research and the multitudes of treatments for thousands and thousands of ailments—almost all of that massive infrastructure is dependent on the lab results. It is almost as if the entire health care industry is dependent on lab results to give it direction.

Considering all of this, the importance of the integrity of lab tests can't be understated. In spite of how important the private and public lab systems are, for the most part they are taken for granted. When everything is going fine, they go unnoticed. But if anything goes wrong, it compromises not only everything in health care, but the Ministry or Department of Health and the governing party.

As an example, in 2005 it was discovered that as many as 1,500 breast cancer lab tests conducted between 1997 and 2005 might have been compromised. These tests were used to determine whether women could benefit from potentially life-saving oncology treatments. The worst-case scenario was that all 1,500 women were directed on a course of treatment that wasn't appropriate to their condition. After retesting, it was discovered that almost 400 lab tests were in error and more than 100 women had to change their course of treatment.

This discovery sent huge shockwaves throughout Newfoundland

and Labrador and the rest of Canada. It was considered to be such a crisis that a judicial inquiry was commissioned to determine how this problem happened. The commission's findings, that the integrity of Newfoundland and Labrador's health care system had been compromised, were a huge embarrassment to the Conservative government of the day, headed by Danny Williams. In addition, a class-action lawsuit was settled for $17 million.

The Institute for Quality Management in Healthcare (IQMH) was created in 1999 by the Ontario Medical Association as a not-for-profit organization to ensure that the work done by private and public labs in Ontario is of the highest quality. It tests both the procedures labs use and the outcomes they produce. The organization is funded by the Ontario government, but that funding may be reduced or eliminated in the coming years.

"This presented a big challenge for us," said Dr. Greg Flynn, CEO and managing director of IQMH. "We had to develop new sources of revenue, and in order to do that, we had to understand and be able to clearly articulate who we are and what is our value to all of our stakeholders. While I had an intuitive understanding of all of this, I couldn't communicate effectively, which means nobody else in the organization could, either. I knew that having a vague notion in my head wasn't enough. It had to be formally expressed and institutionalized so that the selling of the organization wasn't dependent solely on its leader. This is why we did a Blueprint."

When an organization falls down, the ramifications are usually felt far beyond the company. For instance, if Walmart makes a mistake, it certainly hurts the company and maybe its customers as well. But if the problem does extend to customers, it usually represents only an inconvenience or a lack of value—it isn't life- or career-threatening. On the other hand, if the public and private lab systems fail, there are extreme consequences for many stakeholders, not the least of whom are patients who could be misdiagnosed and sent on an incorrect course of treatment that could affect their lives and livelihoods.

As the organization that ensures the credibility of the public and private lab systems, there is a lot of pressure on IQMH to maintain the integrity of lab processes and results. This became the central notion of its Blueprint. Dr. Flynn stated in the Blueprint that it wasn't enough merely to maintain the integrity of the lab system; it had to be constantly improved. Our first pass at a Core Proposition landed us on "Elevating faith in the system." Everyone agreed that the idea was accurate, but most objected to the word *faith* because it was seen as having too much of a religious connotation. We debated the merits of both *confidence* and *integrity* and decided that, at the end of the day, what stakeholders wanted was confidence in the system and it was the integrity of the results that inspired confidence. This is how "Elevating confidence in the system" became the Core Proposition of IQMH.

Before we could finalize IQMH's Core Proposition, we had to make sure that it resonated powerfully with all of the stakeholders, including:

Patients, because the integrity of lab tests could mean the difference between life and death to them.

Employees, because it was the cause to which they were committed and one that gave them a sense of purpose.

Public and private labs, because IQMH provides third-party validation of the quality of their work and, with its *Good Housekeeping* seal of approval, outsiders will know that the labs not only do good work, but are in a constant state of improvement.

Ministry of Health, because having confidence in the lab system was the first step in having confidence in the entire health care system.

Government, because if the integrity of the health care system is compromised, it reflects on the government and becomes a major embarrassment.

Doctors, because the quality of their treatment, and their ability to be good doctors to their patients, is highly dependent on the integrity of lab results.

The Ontario Medical Association, because it is the industry association of Ontario doctors and one of its mandates is to maintain the positive reputation of doctors as a community.

With validation from all these sources, IQMH promoted "Elevating confidence in the system" as its Core Proposition and began a two-part process of shifting some of its operations to be aligned with its mandate and going out to tell the world its new story.

Aboriginal Human Resource Council's Core Proposition

Canada's 1.4 million Aboriginal people have always had a challenging relationship with the rest of Canada. Among other things, they are significantly underrepresented in the workforce, which, in many cases, has had a drastic impact on their quality of life. These impacts include poverty, drug and alcohol abuse, crime, and a lack of education and training.

The negative impacts aren't limited to the Aboriginal community. The resource sector is the engine of Canada's economy, and its need for skilled and unskilled labour is huge. A significant proportion of resource initiatives are either on or close to Aboriginal lands and communities. A healthy, educated and skilled Aboriginal community could alleviate much of the labour shortage in the resource sector.

The Aboriginal Human Resource Council (AHRC) was founded almost two decades ago to help educate and train Aboriginal peoples and to work with companies to facilitate their inclusion in the workforce. The AHRC has developed a variety of services (job fairs, skills training, employment conferences) that help Aboriginal peoples become ready for the workforce and that help companies develop policies, procedures and cultural training to make their workplaces more conducive to Aboriginal employment.

While this sounds like a hand-in-glove business model, the AHRC has struggled to convince corporations of the value of its services. Too many companies participated in AHRC programs at the lowest fee level, doing the minimum amount of work necessary to be seen as Aboriginal-friendly. This has slowed the process of Aboriginal inclusion in the workforce and has starved the AHRC of necessary operating capital.

On the bright side for the Aboriginal community, its negotiating leverage with corporate Canada, particularly in the resource sector, has been increasing by leaps and bounds over the last decade. Any Canadian company that wants to exploit resources on Aboriginal lands has to come to a formal agreement with the Aboriginal communities that own them. If Aboriginal communities don't feel they are getting a fair deal from the resource companies, withholding their approval can cost resource companies as much as tens of millions of dollars. Obviously, it is in the best interest of resource companies to develop contractual relationships with Aboriginal communities as quickly and easily as possible in order for their projects to move forward.

The challenge in consummating these agreements is that the two parties (Aboriginal communities and resource companies) know very little about the workings of each other's cultures. When two companies are negotiating an agreement, it is usually the financial imperative that that drives the discussions. As long as it is a financial win for both companies, the deal usually gets done. While the financial imperative is important to Aboriginal communities, there are other factors that are equally important, such as the ecological preservation of their lands and the social preservation of their cultures. Too many companies, especially in the resource sector, are woefully ignorant of Aboriginal culture. Compounding this problem is that "the Aboriginal community" is not monolithic. It is made up of thousands of tribes and communities, many with their own unique customs and cultures. What is seen as a significant negotiating factor in one Aboriginal community may be of no consequence to a neighbouring community that is a part of the same negotiation for a resource initiative.

This cultural gulf is one of the primary reasons for the failure of negotiations between Aboriginal communities and companies wanting to exploit Canada's natural resources. While it is a frustration for companies and Aboriginal communities alike, it also provides those Aboriginal communities with a significant amount of negotiating leverage. Without their approval, for whatever reason, the resources don't get exploited.

It was this cultural gulf that led to the AHRC's Core Proposition and laid the foundation for its transformation. The AHRC has spent the past 17 years with one foot in corporate Canada and the other in Aboriginal communities, and as a result, it has a deep understanding of the way both operate. This creates the opportunity for it to be the bridge between the two communities as they struggle to create business relationships. It can provide companies with the cultural insight and sensitivity required to forge business relationships with Aboriginal communities. The insight that it brings can accelerate the negotiating process and save companies millions of dollars that would otherwise be lost to delays, work stoppages and protests.

As we explored the notion of Aboriginal leverage and the AHRC's unique position as a potential bridge between these two cultures, it became apparent to us that its future role is to build prosperous commercial relationships between the two parties. "Building prosperous commercial relationships" became its Core Proposition. "We knew we could play a valuable role in the emerging world of Aboriginal leverage," says Kelly Lendsay, CEO of the AHRC. "We just couldn't see, until we discovered our Core Proposition, the magnitude of the value of the skill set we had acquired over the years. Our Core Proposition laid the foundation for a transformation of the AHRC, from an organization providing a variety of à la carte HR services to one that plays a fundamental role in advancing the goals and prosperity of Aboriginal peoples and corporations." This new mandate set the stage for the development of comprehensive consulting services at fees that are commensurate with the millions of dollars of value they bring to resource companies.

Lymphoma Canada's Core Proposition

Cancer is a word that strikes fear in the hearts of most people. While treatment for most cancers has advanced by leaps and bounds over the past decades, for many people it means a death sentence. When people are diagnosed with cancer, they and their loved ones enter a bewildering world characterized by lack of knowledge about the disease and a seemingly byzantine medical system.

The confusion about what to do and what to expect spawned the grassroots development of most cancer support groups. Ordinary people banded together and began to gather information and offer personal support to people living with cancer and their families. At some point in their evolution, informal groups crystallize into not-for-profit organizations run on a shoestring by dedicated volunteers. With effective management, these groups can grow over time into fund-raising and service-delivery behemoths.

This is exactly the path Lymphoma Canada is on. It came to us as a small, underfunded but committed grassroots organization that was ready to expand its ability to help people with lymphoma and their families, as well as its fund-raising capability. In its quest to grow to the next level, it faced a number of challenges:

- Determining exactly what role to play in helping people and families living with lymphoma
- Creating a focus for its activities that is within its fund-raising means
- Developing a compelling story that will raise its profile, its level of influence and its ability to attract corporate and individual donors

We focused on the first point in the development of Lymphoma Canada's Blueprint. In order to determine the most valuable role the organization can play, we had to understand the mindset of people diagnosed with lymphoma and the feelings of their loved ones in order to recognize that the initiatives the organization offered were relevant to the ordeal these people were going through. We were able to explore this on a firsthand basis because most of the people involved in Lymphoma Canada's Blueprint were either living with the disease or a loved one.

We explored in detail what people are thinking and feeling from the moment they suspect something is wrong, through diagnosis and treatment, and ending either with survivorship or the passing of the patient. Fear and confusion were the two words that came up over and over again in this conversation. "Will I live or die?" "What is the best course of action?" "Who in the medical system helps me through this process?" "Why is the medical system so confusing?" "What will I experience, both positive and negative, through the course of treatment?" "What is the best way to support someone who is living with the disease?" "How, as a family member or friend, do I keep myself emotionally strong so I can provide the best support?"

We also asked what the best outcome was for everybody involved. Obviously, part of the answer is that the person with lymphoma lives a long and happy life. Another part of the answer came from people's experience spiralling into depression as a result of their diagnosis. Everyone agreed that this debilitating emotional state was a barrier to successful treatment.

Just as *fear* and *confusion* were the two words that were central to a diagnosis, *power* and *control* were the two words that dominated the discussion about best-case outcomes. Fear and confusion make you feel powerless, which triggers the depression. Knowledge and understanding give you a feeling of control and ultimately hope. The more in control you feel, the more power you have. The more understanding you have about the disease and your course of treatment, the more you will feel in control.

All cancer-support organizations provide lots of information on the disease and what to expect. But to what end? This was the question we needed to answer from the two conversations above. Our discussion involved the nature of the path those with lymphoma follow and their emotional mindset as they navigate that path. Everybody agreed that the more powerful you feel as you go down that path, the more likely it is you will have a positive outcome. It doesn't mean you will be cured if you follow that path powerfully; it just means you and everybody around you will have a more positive experience.

This is how we arrived at Lymphoma Canada's Core Proposition: "Navigating powerfully through the process." The treatment process can be long and arduous. How to navigate the process can be confusing. Lymphoma Canada's specific support role is not only to help you through the process, but to do it in such a way that you feel in control and powerful. This is true both for people living with lymphoma and for their family and friends.

What became apparent from this Core Proposition is that Lymphoma Canada does more than just offer information and support. It now had a much higher objective. It has to guide you through the process in such a way that you feel in control and powerful. This fundamentally impacts how the organization offers information, the kinds of initiatives it develops and the kinds of outcomes people may expect from its work.

5

Core Story

Everyone Singing from the Same Song Sheet

So far, we've explained how your Core Proposition guides everything you do and say as an organization. Then we discussed how you use the Core Proposition to align everything you do—all of the parts of your Business Architecture—with who you are at your core. This gives you a singular operational focus on the one thing that makes you uniquely remarkable. The final step is to use your Core Proposition to guide everything you say.

By "everything you say," we mean how you communicate explicitly and implicitly. Explicit communication usually involves words: the ones that come out of your mouth, that are written on your website, that appear in PowerPoint presentations, that you tweet and post on your blog.

Implicit communication is all the stuff you do that has to be interpreted to mean something. For instance, the Nike swoosh and the Apple apple are examples of logos that need to be interpreted, whereas the Ford logo, which is a wordmark, is an example of explicit communication. (Before you say the Apple logo is just an apple, so it doesn't need to be interpreted, remember that it has a bite taken out of it—and that has meaning!) You can see an example of implicit communication in our Blueprint logo as well. If you don't know that our Core Proposition is "From confusion to clarity," our logo doesn't make a lot of sense. But as soon as you know our Core Proposition, you can see that our logo is a literal interpretation of that.

Other examples of implicit communication are package design and the graphic style you use for visual advertising (such as magazine ads, television partials or web layout). Using Apple as an example again, take any Apple print ad or packaging, remove the logo and change the language to Swahili, and as an English-speaking person you will still recognize it as representing Apple.

The reason we're placing such emphasis on implicit communication is because it isn't as obvious that it communicates who you are as much as spoken and printed words do. Design and pictures speak as much about who you are as words do, so what they say to the outside world and your employees needs to be guided by your Core Proposition as much as words do.

What Your Core Story Isn't

As we go through the process of showing you how to construct your Core Story, it is important to understand what it isn't as well as what it is. Your Core Story is not advertising copy of any kind. It won't appear in brochures or in PowerPoint presentations. You won't hear a voiceover in a TV commercial reading the Core Story. You won't see the Core Story in magazine or newspaper copy, nor will it appear on any blogs.

What Your Core Story Is

While it isn't any of the things we've outlined above, it *is* the guide for all of those things. When we say that your Core Story guides everything you say, we mean *everything*. If you are a consumer packaged-goods company, your package design firm should be as versed in your Blueprint as your advertising agency, your web design firm, your public relations house and any other group, internal or external, that is generating any kind of communications materials for you. Since every one of those communications pieces is an expression of who you are, it should be guided by your Core Story, the construction of which is guided by your Core Proposition. It is a logical progression from the core out. Everything that you say on the outside is an expression of who you are on the inside.

Your Core Story is the explanation of your Core Proposition, from the logic of why this is valuable, to where it came from, to the methodology you employ to make it happen. We develop your Core Story from six different angles. In order:

Who are you? The first answer is the simplest and most obvious. It is the expression of who you are, and it is answered with the name of your organization and your Core Proposition.

What does (your Core Proposition) mean? The explanation that is developed is the Core Logic of your Core Proposition.

Why are you qualified to do (what your Core Proposition says)? The third step assumes that it's fine and dandy to say that this is who you are, but now you have to explain why you're qualified to do what you say.

What is your methodology? By now, we think you're legit . . . in theory. But can you deliver? We need to hear about your unique methodology in order to believe that you can pull it off.

What are the beliefs that lead you to (your Core Proposition)? Now we want to know where your Core Proposition came from. What are the beliefs (not the values) that led you to this place?

What do I get as a result of (your Core Proposition)? Finally, what's in it for me? If I buy your service or product, what do I get?

The first question—"Who are you?"—has a short answer: name and Core Proposition. If you were to try to answer any of the other questions now, it would probably take you 15 to 20 minutes of rambling. In this time your audience's eyes will glaze over. People will be constantly checking their watches, glancing at the door and wondering how quickly they can bolt from the room.

The goal is to reduce every one of these answers from 15 to 20 minutes down to between four and eight bullet points. When somebody asks you a complex question like "What is your methodology?" (usually asked as "What do you do and how do you do it differently?"), you will be able to provide a crisp, compelling answer in one or two minutes. Not only will people get it, and get the value to them immediately, but none of your competitors will be able to talk in such a concise way about their businesses, their products or their services. Your story will stand out like a compelling beacon in an ocean of banality.

Let's go through each of the sections one at a time and look at real-life examples of how they are answered.

Who Are You?

A Core Proposition never floats out there on its own because it has no meaning as a solitary phrase. When you hear a Core Proposition like "An easier way," if you don't know that the company is Deluxe

Toronto and the industry it operates in is movie and TV production, you wouldn't have a clue what it means. Or you would think it was too generic. On the other hand, if a person at a broadcast conference introduces himself by saying, "I'm from Deluxe Toronto and I help producers find an easier way," his audience gets what he's saying because they have the context of knowing both the company and the industry.

It's a bit of an extreme example, but if the same person is at a shoe conference and says, "I'm from Deluxe Toronto and I help producers find an easier way," nobody is going to know the value of "An easier way" because they don't know Deluxe Toronto, they don't know the production business and they don't know the hardships of being a movie producer. But none of this matters. The person from Deluxe Toronto doesn't care if people in the shoe business don't get him, because they will never be customers of his. Generalizing this thought, it doesn't matter if your Core Proposition means nothing to people outside of the field in which your company operates, because you will never do business with them. Your Core Proposition has to have meaning and resonance only inside your sphere of business.

What this illustrates is that there are always two contexts in which a Core Proposition is presented, with one being expressed and the other implied. The expressed context is the name of the company. If you are in a related field, you know what Deluxe Toronto does, and that gives meaning to the Core Proposition "An easier way." The implied context is the industry in which Deluxe Toronto, its customers and suppliers and its strategic partners operates. In our example with the broadcast conference, Deluxe Toronto is having these conversations about who it is with people who are familiar with the industry.

All of this is to explain why, when creating your story, the question "Who are you?" is always answered with the name of the company and its Core Proposition. The name of the company gives meaning to the Core Proposition because people within your sphere of business know what your company does and know the field in which you operate.

If you recall, near the end of chapter 3 we introduced this relationship to you:

Say the Core Proposition → *Understand the Core Logic* → *Feel the Emotional Impact*

Answering the question "Who are you?" expresses the Core Proposition. Next, we'll deal with the Core Logic and Emotional Resonance with the question "What does that mean?"

What Does That Mean?

This is often the toughest question to answer in the Core Story, because the Core Proposition can mean so much if you try to explain everything about it. So the key here is to boil it down to the Core Logic. What is the absolute minimum you can say in order to have somebody understand and feel what it means?

We'll start by looking at our own company, Blueprint. Let's examine Blueprint's Core Proposition—"From confusion to clarity"—and then deconstruct it to understand how to attack this question.

Who are you?
Blueprint. "From confusion to clarity."

What does that mean?

1. CEOs are often faced with an overabundance of conflicting information about where to take the company they lead.

- Members of the board and executive team will each have their own opinions and will likely be lobbying the CEO to adopt their point of view.
- There is often a large volume of market research that points its fingers in many different directions.

2. With so many competing options and what seems like such strong rationale to choose each one, the CEO is often left confused about how to make the best decision for the company.

3. Although there can be many viable options, business discipline and responsible use of budgets force the CEO to choose just one direction.

4. Blueprinting creates a single, compelling focus for an organization by defining who it is at its core in seven words or less.

5. This single focus becomes the decision-making filter for everyone in the organization, guiding every decision they may make and every action they take.

You can probably imagine that there is a lot more we could say here. In a new business conversation, we describe what we do in a lot more detail than just these five points and two sub-points. But all we're trying to get across in the Core Story is the Core Logic of the business.

Now let's analyze what we've written above. There are two parts to the answer to the question "What does that mean?"

- The context for what you do. Another way to say that: it is the problem you are solving.
- What you do to solve the problem.

In the example of Blueprint's Core Proposition, the problem is defined by the first three points plus the two subpoints: the CEO has a multitude of viable options for the direction of the company; many of those options seem to lead to excellent future opportunities for company. How do you choose just one?

You may be wondering how you identify the core problem that your company solves for your clients. Since the Core Story is the last thing we do in the creation of a Blueprint, by this time there will have been many hours of conversation about the business, the market in which it operates, the needs of its customers and what it does for them. We just take information that has been identified previously and distill it down to simple and concise language.

The last two points in the Blueprint example are what we do to solve the CEO's problem:

- Blueprinting defines who you are your core.
- The articulation of your core becomes the basis for all decision making.

The Core Logic appeals to a CEO's frustration and possibly even their embarrassment. The Emotional Resonance alleviates the frustration or anger and creates hope (from the frustration of confusion to the hope and opportunity clarity brings, to make our Core Proposition a little bit more verbose).

Answering this question explains in a nutshell what you do. We've stripped away all of the extraneous and qualifying information about what we do and articulated it in its simplest form. What we're trying to achieve in this answer is the reaction, "Interesting. I get it. Now tell me more." Both the logic that is expressed in this answer and the emotional impact that is implied build intrigue in what you do. The prospect begins to understand not only your business, but also its personal value. That's just a beginning, however; more information is required, and that will be covered off in answering the other questions. But before we move on, let's look at some other examples of answers to the question "What does that mean?"

Let's consider the answer of Elevate, an online publishing service:

Who are you?
Elevate. "Elevate your credibility."

What does that mean?

1. How effectively you sell yourself or your business is based on your credibility.
2. One of the most powerful ways to increase your credibility is by publishing (books, columns, blog posts).
3. The challenge with publishing is it takes a long time to generate original material that will be perceived as valuable by your audiences.
4. We elevate your credibility by making it faster and easier to find relevant content generated by others and publish it online to the target groups that are critical to your sales.
5. Our online publishing service encourages people to share your content with their networks, greatly expanding the distribution of your content and providing you with third-party endorsement or validation.

Elevate's answer follows the same pattern as ours. There are five points, the first three of which establish the context for the answer, or the problem Elevate is solving. In this case, it boils down to:

- Publish to increase your credibility, but it's difficult.
- We make it fast and easy for you to publish to a continuously expanding audience.

The Core Logic transforms a lingering, latent fear into hope and ego gratification.

Let's look at another longer example; a wealth management firm for individuals, with a unique approach.

Who are you?
Emeritus Financial Strategies. "Following the smart money."

What does that mean?

1. **There are two broad factors that need to be considered when designing an effective financial strategy:**
   - How you create a financial plan, how you grow your wealth and how you draw it down, usually after you retire.
   - There are generally two kinds of long-term market cycles: consistent growth, as we had from 1980 to 2000, and consistent flat or decline, which we have been in since 2000 and which is projected to continue for the foreseeable future.
2. **Your investment strategy in each cycle—how you grow your wealth—is different because what is effective in one cycle is detrimental in the other.**
   - For instance, buy and hold is commonly perceived as an effective and safe investment strategy, but it will actually lose money in a flat or declining market.
3. **There are two problems with mainstream financial planning and investment:**
   - The investment strategies designed for a consistent growth cycle are being improperly advocated in a flat or declining cycle because this is where the investment community (banks, fund companies, advisors) makes its highest profits and easiest sales.
   - It is critically important to have an effective strategy for drawing down your money to protect your wealth. In spite of this

importance, very few investment professionals have developed plans to draw down their clients' wealth effectively.

4. A minority of investors—the "smart money"—can afford to hire teams of dedicated analysts to assess the market for them, tailor their investment strategies to the characteristics of the current long-term market cycle, and have a disciplined strategy for how to effectively draw it down.

5. We observe what the smart money is doing, when it is doing it, and steer our clients into the same strategies (for both growth and drawdown) so that their money works harder and lasts longer.

In spite of what it may look like, there is no rule of fives to answer "What does this mean?", even though the three examples we've given (Blueprint, Elevate, Emeritus) all have five major supporting points.

We wanted to include the Core Logic for Emeritus because it is unusually long. But you can see that it follows the same pattern: What is the context or problem, and what do we do to solve it?

- There are two critical factors in the management of your money that nobody is telling you about.
- Virtually the only people who are taking these factors into account are those who are rich enough to afford their own teams of analysts and planners (they are the smart money).
- We watch what they do and do the same for you.

This Core Logic appeals to fear (for your money) and anger (that you haven't been informed about these critical issues). This fear and anger lie dormant inside you waiting to be tapped. It surfaces when you hear a story built around a very simple, and very real, logic. It makes you perk up your ears and say, "Wait a minute, tell me more. I had no idea." When you hear the Core Logic, the fear and anger are transformed into hope because of the possibility that you will have the same advantages as the smart money.

As a potential customer, if you buy the Core Logic to the extent that you feel the Emotional Resonance, the next thing you want to know is "Can you deliver for me?" The question we ask to get to that answer is "Why are you qualified to do that?"

Why Are You Qualified to Do That?

What is the substance behind who you are as individuals or as a company that gives you the credentials to uniquely fulfill your Core Proposition and its underlying Core Logic? The purpose of this section is to satisfy the questioner that you can actually do what you say you can do. You've proven you can talk the talk; now prove that you can walk the walk.

To begin to answer this question, let's pick up where we left off in the previous section with Emeritus Financial Strategies.

Why are you qualified to do that?

- I am a Certified Financial Planner (CFP).
- I have a Level 2 certification for life insurance planning and sales.
- I have been a financial planner for 19 years, and was one of the top advisors at a major national investment firm for 17 years, during which time I became disillusioned with the industry's propensity to provide advice that maximized its profitability even though it often wasn't in the best interest of the customer.
- I have a more comprehensive understanding of personal tax and tax planning than most investment advisors and financial planners.

- I have an MBA from the Schulich School of Business at York University.
- I spent 16 years in strategic planning in the packaged-goods business (Campbell Foods, Quaker Oats), which gave me experience in, and an appreciation of, a disciplined, objective process for determining what to do.
- Unlike the majority of people and companies in the financial advice community, I am not tied to any particular products, compensation format or investment strategy, so I am free to do what is ethically in the best interests of my clients.
- There are two personal factors that motivated me to follow this investment path:
  - I left a very lucrative career, so I have the freedom to do only what is in the best interests of my clients.
  - I want to do for my clients only what I am doing for myself.

This is an unusually long answer for the question, but only because the founder of this company has such incredible credentials. You'll notice that most of them are technical, such as experience in the industry, certifications, university degrees and related outside experience. Also included are the two personal factors at the end, because although they are not tangible and measurable like the rest of the points, they do speak to credibility. You have to be careful when adding personal factors such as these, because in theory you can add a whole lot of them that sound wonderful and mean nothing. What gives meaning to these personal factors is the sacrifice he made by leaving a very lucrative career so that he could take this more altruistic path.

Now let's look at Eckler, the defined-benefit pension firm, whose current customer base won't exist in the next five to ten years. To its credit, although it has a number of very lucrative years ahead before this market dries up, Eckler recognized that it has to start now to create a new future to replace the one that is disappearing. Waiting another two or three years before it begins this process likely would've meant starting too late and having to downsize during its transition. By starting now, the firm will hopefully be able to maintain its consistent level of growth.

This firm specializes in a very specific field of pensions. All of its thinking for decades has revolved around this kind of pension. Eckler defines itself as both actuaries and pension consultants. But as we mentioned above, the kind of pension work it specializes in is disappearing. So, what to do next?

Actuaries create mathematical models that help pension managers understand future conditions, enabling them to best manage their programs. They gather the data, run the numbers, analyze the projected outcomes and make recommendations to mitigate risk. At least, that's how an actuary would explain it to you.

In a quest to understand the real value Eckler brings to its clients, we had a conversation that we paraphrase like this:

US. Your clients, the CEO and the CFO have to make critical decisions now about what large sums of money will do in the future.
THEM. Right.
US. And the models you create, and the conclusions you draw from them, help them make better decisions now about what the money is going to do in the future.
THEM. Right.
US. And you have given us these three compelling reasons why the models you make are better than those of your competitors.
THEM. Right.
US. So it sounds like you are in the business of predicting the future.
THEM. *Wrong!* Nobody can predict the future.
US. It's true that nobody can predict the future with certainty. But you can predict the future *with a greater degree of certainty.*

THEM. What do you mean?

US. Imagine you are the brand manager of Tide in the U.S. You spend $500 million a year growing the brand. To meet next year's objectives, you feel you need $550 million—a $50 million increase in budget. What if that number should really be $700 million? Or what if it should be $300 million? In the first instance, you are spending $150 million too little, which would make your $550 million inefficient. In the second instance, you are spending *a quarter of a billion dollars* too much!

THEM. We could help them do that easily!

US. Right! You are giving them a greater degree of certainty about what their budget should be.

They struggled for a while with the idea that their Core Proposition could be "A greater degree of certainty," mostly because they kept hearing it as "certainty." But after they heard more examples that weren't related to pensions and realized how well the Core Proposition fit with pensions, too, they not only became comfortable with it, they actually became inspired by it.

This gave them the conceptual framework they needed to look for new kinds of business. When they define themselves as actuaries or pension specialists, their world is narrow and getting narrower by the day. By defining themselves as "A greater degree of certainty," all they have to do to find new business is look out into the marketplace, look for uncertainty of any kind, look for CEOs who are suffering as a result of the uncertainty they are feeling, and tell them that Eckler can create mathematical models that will give them a greater degree of certainty around the important business decision that is causing them angst.

The question then becomes: Why are they uniquely qualified to deliver on the promise of "A greater degree of certainty"? Let's look at their answer.

Why are you qualified to do that?

1. We are academically trained and professionally experienced in our core service, which is the design of mathematical models, the interpretation of data and the formulation of recommendations.
2. We are able to apply our technical experience with more creativity than our competitors because we only hire senior people who:
   - Have a level of ingenuity that produces a higher degree of creativity when generating models, interpreting what they produce and developing recommendations.
   - Are far more involved in every aspect of the service delivery process, from top to bottom, so their creativity is applied to our client work more broadly and deeply.
3. As a partner-owned firm competing against companies that are accountable to individual and institutional shareholders, we have the flexibility to customize solutions to each specific client situation.
   - This brings a greater degree of rigour and good judgment to client solutions.
   - The cookie-cutter models of our competitors are more beneficial to driving revenue than to determining the most valuable solutions for clients.

In analyzing this answer, the first point states that we have the cost of entry: Eckler's people are professionally trained and certified, and they have lots of experience in their field. This is not meant to be a differentiating point, but it does speak to their qualifications. The second point states that because of its creativity and hands-on approach (two important distinguishing factors relative to the companies it competes against), this company is able to bring a higher degree of creativity to the creation of models, the interpretation of the results and the development of recommendations. And finally, not being accountable to shareholders allows the company the flexibility to do the right thing for its clients. As evidence of this last point, when they answer the next question about their Core Beliefs, one of them states, "If there is a choice between quality and profitability, we will choose quality every time."

In the first three Core Story questions, we examined who your organization is, what it does and what qualifications you have to actually deliver on that promise.

What Is Your Methodology?

We believe that every company started for the same reason: an individual or a group of people said, "I know a better way to do this." Often they were working in a particular field, they gained experience and the perspective on how business should be done in that field, and when they reached a breaking point about how it was being done or they saw an opportunity, they left to start their own business according to a unique philosophy that had been gestating in them over the years. How they do it differently could entail a minor modification of how they've done it before, or it could be that they are leveraging a new technology to create a substantial shift in how that product or service is delivered.

A statement like "I know a better way to do this" is just the tip of the iceberg for an incredible amount of thinking that has gone on inside that person's head or inside the heads of the people who created the company together.

One of the products of that thinking is the organization's unique methodology. Every company has a unique methodology, whether they know it or not, that is derived from the statement "I know a better way to do this." If everyone who starts a business has a unique take on how that business should run, it follows logically that every company has a unique methodology.

With respect to methodology, clients either know what theirs is when they begin their Blueprint or they don't. If they know what it is, it gives us a big head start in our discussion. However, most companies don't know what their unique methodology is, so we have to either discover it or define it in the Blueprint. We know that most companies don't know their unique methodology; when they pitch business, they either speak in vague generalities or describe features and benefits that are true of everyone in their category. In essence, they are pitching what their *category* does, not what *they* do.

Companies often feel an incredible sense of relief when they discover or define their unique methodology. For the first time, they understand and can explain exactly how they do what they do, and they can see specifically how it differs from their competitors. We often hear, "I knew we did things differently; we just couldn't explain it in a way that didn't sound generic."

If the company already has a sound, unique methodology that has just been better articulated in the Blueprint, it doesn't usually have to make any immediate shifts to that part of the business. However, as we will see momentarily with Lymphoma Canada, the methodology was developed *in* Blueprint, so it needs to be built from the ground up. This is not a process of starting from scratch, because much of the work it had been doing was still relevant and fit within the methodology. But there was still a substantial amount of work to be done to build this new methodology.

Let's look at Lymphoma Canada's methodology.

Lymphoma Canada provides an online navigation tool that:
- Maps out the path (with key stages and milestones), helping you navigate the process

- Provides extensive information on each stage and key milestones so that patients know what to expect, common setbacks, the right questions to ask, treatment options, etc.
- Is a resource that is with you every step of the way, whenever and wherever you need it

The navigation tool guides you through each stage of the disease:
- Pre-diagnosis
- Diagnosis
- Treatment (including "watch and wait")
- Post-treatment
- Relapse (if necessary)
- Retreatment
- Palliative care (if necessary)
- Survivorship at all stages of the experience

The purpose of the navigation tool is to provide patients and their caregivers with:
- A full understanding of the disease, the treatment process and their options
- A sense of control and confidence

As we said, this is a new methodology, so much of it needs to be created. This will be a big job for the management team at Lymphoma Canada because they have to identify all of the steps on the path, determine all of the characteristics of each step, figure out what support they are going to provide in each step, slot in the existing information and resources where they fit on the new path, and then determine what information, resources and initiatives need to be developed to fill in the gaps in the path.

Now let's look at Momentum's methodology. An additional point you need in order to understand Momentum's methodology is that the company isn't just building condos which cater to the most essential needs of downsizers; it is creating these developments on properties that are owned by branches of the Royal Canadian Legion. The Legion is a nonprofit organization that serves veterans, mostly of the Second World War. Because there are so few veterans still alive, Legion membership is dwindling and its branches' economic viability is threatened. Many Legion halls are on prime real estate, such as waterfront properties.

Drew McDougall, CEO of Momentum, is creating partnerships with these Legion branches whereby he buys their land and the condo he builds will have a Legion hall inside. The Legion members gain revenue from the sale of the land, a modern permanent home within a broader community, and economic viability. Drew gains a prime piece of real estate that is attractive to downsizers.

Legions as Locations
- There are 1,500 Legions in Canada, many of which are excellent locations for residences.
- Due to declining membership, Legions are open to conversations about development, provided their community/programming needs are addressed.
- The residences we build on Legion lands will have a component that addresses the future needs of Legions and their members so that the organization is sustainable.

Residences and Podiums
- The residences themselves will be attractive, from both an aesthetic and price standpoint, to upper-middle-class buyers.
- The podium (the base of each building) will house two types of facilities:
  - A space dedicated to the Legion

- Services that provide essential needs for the downsizer
  residents
- The services in the podium (medical offices, restaurant, yoga/
  spa, pharmacy, etc.) will all provide services to the residents
  (e.g., meals delivered to condos) as well as to the surrounding
  community.

Lifestyle Model

- The residents will have an interest in proactive management
  of their wellness.
- Momentum will provide two services in the podium that
  cater to the wellness needs of residents:
  - Retailers and facilities that cater to wellness needs (e.g., health
    care professionals, yoga/spa)
  - A life concierge who will help navigate and coordinate residents'
    needs for wellness, health, leisure and other services

There is a fundamental difference between Lymphoma Canada's methodology and Momentum's, aside from the fact that they operate in two entirely different worlds. For the most part, Lymphoma Canada's methodology has yet to be developed because it is new. Momentum's unique methodology was already in place prior to its Blueprint. In fact, the conversation in Momentum's Blueprint process was driven by its methodology. As we said before, when a company comes to us with a unique methodology already in place, it makes the development of the Blueprint easier. But it is rare to find a company, existing or new, that has a well-defined, well-articulated methodology.

Bloom Burton is the investment bank that helps emerging health care and biotech companies achieve a faster path to their monetizing event. Its very simple six-part methodology, which supports all of the financing aspects necessary to achieve a faster path to monetization, is set out below.

1. Deeper Level of Due Diligence

Bloom Burton's team of dedicated and specialized professionals investigates investee companies to verify opportunities and expose risks. For every investment or project, our team investigates:

- Basic science/mechanism of action
- Pre-clinical data
- Clinical strategy and execution
- Regulatory path
- Intellectual property
- Business and commercialization plans
- Manufacturing and CMC (Canadian Management Centre) considerations
- Valuation
- Financing strategy
- Management capabilities

2. Wider Range of Financing Options

Bloom Burton has considerable experience across the broadest range of funding options available, including:

- Traditional equity and debt financing
- Convertible and hybrid structures
- Royalty financing
- Strategic partnering and investments
- Government and non-dilutive financing

Bloom Burton also has experience working with both private and public companies at all stages of development, from start-up through multinational, and with companies operating in all areas of health care, including biotechnology, pharmaceutical, medical device, diagnostic, health care services, health care IT, life science tools, animal health, and nutrition and wellness.

3. Wider Range of Jurisdictions

Our global experience allows us to consider the widest range of funding options for the companies we represent. Bloom Burton can:

- Attract international health care investors to fund companies of all sizes and stages
- Attract strategic or partnering investments from around the globe
- Guide Canadian and international companies to list on NASDAQ or equivalent exchanges
- Facilitate listing and funding through our local Toronto Stock Exchange, even for non-Canadian companies
- Utilize our in-house knowledge of the technical requirements for funding, listing and selling companies globally

4. Relationships with Health Care–Specialist Investors

- Our team has a long history of working with health care–specialized investor funds.
- These premium relationships with investment thought leaders allow us to gather important market intelligence, understand investment trends and preferences, and test ideas before launching a transaction.
- We have set up thousands of institutional meetings with hundreds of investment funds.
- Our relationships span venture capital, private equity, crossover funds, hedge funds, mutual funds, government agencies, strategic investors and investors that issue debt, monetize royalties or invest via alternative/hybrid structures.

5. Health Care Sector Engagement

- We know more than just companies and investors.
- We regularly speak with academic researchers, universities and medical schools, technology transfer and incubator organizations, angel groups, policy makers and government. We also serve on the boards of directors of several medical and health care foundations and industry organizations, and we participate on expert panels discussing issues relevant to our sector.
- Our research and analysis appear regularly at events and in the media, and through our own equity research, publications and blog posts. We host Canada's most important investor conference each year, in addition to seminars and symposia to educate and connect the entire industry.
- These activities and others align us closely with all kinds of health care leaders and help keep us, and our clients, attuned to the latest developments in the health care community.

6. Creativity and Tenacity

- We never blame "market conditions" or approach trans-actions as a "numbers game."
- Our long-term commitment to each investor and company challenges us to continuously refine our strategies until we achieve success. We are creative in our approach to financing and growth, and tenacious in finding the right transaction for all parties.

Let's look at a couple of key aspects of Bloom Burton's methodology, beginning with the first point: a deeper level of due diligence. The person leading Bloom Burton's team of analysts was rated as the top analyst in the country in health care and biotech. So any company in which Bloom Burton is investing or for which it is finding investors will have undergone a rigorous examination of the quality of its idea, its management team and the market it is entering. This review will give potential investors a greater degree of confidence in their investment, and passing this tough test acts as a *Good Housekeeping* seal of approval for the health care/biotech company. Bloom Burton hosts the biggest annual Canadian health care/biotech conference that investors and young companies alike from around the world attend.

Point number two is also worth a closer look. Does Bloom Burton offer a broader range of financing options than the big banks it competes against? No. But the big banks are structured along operating lines. This means that each kind of financing is contained within its own business unit. If you are an emerging company in the health care/biotech space and are dealing with the bank for your financing options, you have to create a relationship with a separate business unit at the bank for each kind of financing. Each business unit has its own profit-and-loss requirements and is accountable for growing its own line of business. It can be challenging for these diverse business units within a bank to work together to come up with the right blend of financing for a company. It's known as the "silo problem."

At Bloom Burton, all financing options are under one roof and are managed by the same person. Also, that one person at Bloom Burton has his or her eye on the bigger picture—guiding the company to its monetizing event and not just providing a single form of financing. This allows for a more holistic and integrated approach to the planning and execution of your financing, ensuring that the client ends up with funding that is in its best interest.

Finally, let's look at Elevate's methodology for elevating your credibility.

1. We send to you, in digest form, content that is relevant to you and your clients.

2. We give you the ability to choose the content you want to publish and to provide commentary on the selected content to establish your expertise on the topic.

3. We distribute the content through your email newsletter, Twitter, LinkedIn, Facebook, blog posts and other online publishing channels.

4. We measure how much your audience engages with your published content (what was read, what was passed along to others, etc.).

5. We conduct comprehensive diagnostics to determine how to make sales come faster and easier.

Point number one describes how Elevate helps you find the content you want to publish under your name. You give Elevate categories of content (for instance, "strategy for Blueprint") and it gives you a list of articles on a daily basis related to those categories. In point number two, you select the content you want to publish and then personalize it by writing a couple of sentences or a paragraph about why you think it is relevant to your audience. Point number three explains how the content is then automatically distributed to a variety of online channels that you identify when you set up your account. Point number four describes how Elevate tracks the journey of your published content so that it can deliver on point number five. Point number five is very illuminating and exciting: Elevate feeds back to you who looked at your content and whether or not they passed it along to others. This gives you the opportunity to generate sales by understanding the reading interests of specific members of your audience. For instance, if you are one of the big accounting firms and you notice an audit client is reading content on taxation, it gives you the opportunity to open up a dialogue between the client and tax consultants in your firm.

What Are Your Core Beliefs?

A longer version of this question is "What do you believe in that led you to arrive at your Core Proposition and everything that it means?" Before we go into the specific answer in more detail, let's back up for a second.

As we mentioned, we believe every company starts for the same reason: because somebody says, "I know how to do this better." Encourage that person to talk about what underlies "I know a better way to do that" by asking the following provocative questions:

> What do you really hate about how this business was done in the past?

> If you were a benevolent dictator and could decree how this kind of business should operate, what would you say?

Many of the answers you receive to these questions will take the form of beliefs about how a category should operate. When we asked these questions of our actuary clients, this is one of the answers they gave us:

> *It drives us crazy the way the big firms create these cookie-cutter solutions that maximize their profitability. They are constantly taking client problems and trying to shoehorn them into one of their cookie-cutter solutions so that they can make sure they are operating as efficiently as possible in making the maximum amount of money from the client. In a conflict between profitability and quality, quality should win out every time.*

If you analyze this statement, you can see it contains answers to both of the guiding questions above. The first two sentences answer the question about what they hate about how actuarial services are typically delivered. The last sentence answers the question about what they would do if they were benevolent dictators controlling the actuarial industry.

Instead of saying, "This is how the industry should operate," the actuarial firm said, "This is how *we* should operate." "In a conflict between profitability and quality, quality will win out every time" became one of the firm's Core Beliefs, around which it structured a whole constellation of behaviours. That is the beauty of Core Beliefs: when they are developed accurately, they are so effective in guiding specific, differentiated behaviours, both for individuals and for the organization as a whole.

We often get asked why we don't believe in core values. While some companies develop and apply them very well, most don't. Like vision and mission statements, core values are usually developed and then forgotten. Companies will often use expressions such as "our core values," but they don't actually know what they are, let alone apply them in any meaningful way. We did an online search of companies who express their core values on their websites and found there is a standard list of ten, from which most organizations choose five or six:

Honesty
Accountability
Responsibility
Trust
Reliability
Respect
Co-operation

Customer service
Creativity
Innovation

There are three problems with this list:

1. If most companies adhere to mostly the same values, how will following those values guide them in differentiating themselves?
2. The last three (customer service, creativity and innovation) aren't even values, yet countless companies cite them as core values.
3. For the ones that *are* values, shouldn't all people just operate that way? Aren't most people already honest, trustworthy and cooperative? And if they aren't, why are you hiring them? Aren't these values the cost of entry into the human race?

What we will demonstrate in defining a company's Core Beliefs is that, while no one Core Belief is differentiating, in the aggregate they will create guiding behaviours that will uniquely define the organization and how it operates.

Let's look at an example from Emeritus Financial Strategies. In answering the question "Why are you qualified to do that?" the founder of Emeritus said:

I have been a financial planner for 19 years, and was one of the top advisors at a major national investment firm for 17 years, during which time I became disillusioned with the industry's propensity to provide advice that maximized its profitability even though it often wasn't in the best interest of the customer.

What he is describing is what he hates about how his industry operates. Just as with the actuaries, it is companies that sacrifice the needs of the customer for the sake of their own profitability. From that statement of disgust came the Core Belief:

The development of an effective financial strategy must be totally independent of the profitability of the products that are a part of the plan.

Emeritus built its whole financial management strategy (its behaviour) around this Core Belief: it follows the smart money. In essence, Emeritus is a divining rod for smart money on behalf of its clients. Wherever the smart money goes, Emeritus leads its clients there as well. As soon as Emeritus is not where the smart money is, it will abandon that product and move all of its clients over to where the smart money is *now*. Emeritus has no allegiance to any one product; only the best interests of its customers.

Here are the Core Beliefs that led Emeritus to "Following the smart money":

- The best strategy for planning, investment and redemption is based on the objective characteristics of the long-term market we are in, which takes one of two forms:
  - Overall consistent growth, even though there are ups and downs in the short term
  - Overall flat or declining growth, also with ups and downs in the short term
- Buy and hold, and the products that support it, is a money-losing strategy in an overall flat or declining market cycle.
- An intelligent form of market timing is the most effective financial strategy in an overall flat or declining market.

- The development of an effective financial strategy must be totally independent of the profitability of the products that are a part of the execution of that strategy.
- The more investors' poor decision making can be removed from the financial management process, the more they will make.
- An objective, comprehensive financial plan—knowing *exactly* who you are and where you need to be—is the most important part of the process because it optimizes the performance of the investment and redemption elements of financial management.
- As much intelligence and care must be taken in the development of a drawdown plan in the post-retirement phase as is applied to growing the money in the pre-retirement phase.

Let's see what the entire set of Core Beliefs looks like for AdBuzz, an impressive young start-up whose Core Proposition is "Nurturing the next generation" of advertising professionals. To accomplish this goal, it created a series of online and off-line tools to bridge the gap between advertising schools and advertising agencies. This gap exists because advertising schools in universities and colleges are relatively new and have not yet developed strong relationships with the industry they feed.

A team of young advertising students led by Tom Ritchie saw the difficulty their fellow students were having in breaking into the advertising field. It wasn't that there was a shortage of opportunities; it was just that the agencies didn't know where to look for emerging, trained talent. You can see below that the fallout from this disconnect is captured in the Core Beliefs that led to AdBuzz's Core Proposition, "Nurturing the next generation":

- There should be a strong and direct relationship between the schools that produce marketing communications professionals and the companies that hire them.

- Students should be more informed about all aspects of the industry they want to work in and should play a more active role in getting hired.
- Marketing communications companies should have more awareness of the talent pool of graduating students.
- Marketing communications companies should make a greater effort to nurture entry-level talent.
- The process to get into a creative industry should be creative and fun.
- The industry needs a formal resource for hiring at the entry level because it is not profitable for traditional recruiters to place graduating students.
- Creating more awareness of the breadth of graduating talent will increase the competition for it, which will in turn decrease the ability of employers to have unpaid internships.

When you look at the entire constellation of AdBuzz's products, services and programming, you see they are a direct consequence of these Core Beliefs. In other words, the behaviours of the individuals in the organization and the organization as a whole as they develop services are directly motivated and guided by their Core Beliefs.

The Aboriginal Human Resources Council (AHRC) transformed itself from an organization providing a variety of HR services at relatively low fees to a consulting group committed to "Building prosperous commercial relationships" between Aboriginal peoples and mainstream companies. Its foundational belief is that Aboriginal peoples and corporate Canada will both increase their prosperity through greater Aboriginal inclusion. As you read through the list of the AHRC's Core Beliefs, you can see this notion reflected in each and every one of them. The Core Beliefs also reflect the passionate desire of all of the AHRC's staff to increase the personal, social and financial well-being of Canada's Aboriginal peoples.

- There is untapped financial potential in win-win relationships between corporations and Canada's indigenous peoples.
- Societal attitudes towards indigenous peoples can be improved through social, financial and employment inclusion.
- The more economic activity that can be generated between companies and indigenous people, the more the financial/ education/social/health gap between indigenous society and the rest of Canada can be closed.
- It is more time-efficient and cost-effective to have agreements with indigenous peoples brokered by us than for corporations to do them alone.
- Unlike traditional business deals, which are based mostly on economic benefit, deals with indigenous communities need to factor in cultural and social nuances as well.
- To be an effective facilitator of relationships between corporate Canada and indigenous peoples, we need to have credibility with, and the trust of, both parties.
- There is a bigger trust gap between indigenous peoples and the rest of Canada that must be addressed in order to create effective relationships.
- Forging a relationship between companies and indigenous peoples requires reconciling two cultures that have fundamentally different beliefs, practices and desires.

One of the key questions that had to be addressed in the Blueprint was whether or not the AHRC's existing services should continue to be offered. Remember, the challenge with these services was that the fees they charged were not enough to sustain the organization. What articulating its Core Beliefs demonstrated was that all of the services the AHRC offered in the past are consistent with these beliefs. Although its Core Beliefs weren't articulated before the creation of its Blueprint, they existed within the culture of the organization. Now that they have been articulated, they have both validated the relevance of these services and are guiding the development of new ones.

The most important of the new services is the development of a management consulting-style capability that will have a single focus: bridging the gap between corporate Canada and Aboriginal peoples in order to develop agreements that build prosperous commercial relationships for both sides. Since accelerating the development of these agreements will save companies millions of dollars and will generate millions in revenue for Aboriginal communities, the AHRC will be able to charge consulting fees that are consistent with the value they bring; this will subsidize its historical HR services, which are valuable but can't command the same level of fees.

What Do I Get?

In the summer of 2014, we were two sessions into a client's Blueprint and were having a conversation to reveal its Core Proposition. The CEO said, "Our target groups and stakeholders are so varied, I don't get how we can have one Core Proposition that resonates with all of them." We reminded her to trust the process; to her credit, she did. Less than half an hour later we discovered her Core Proposition. The moment it popped out in the conversation, she smiled and said, "Now I get it."

While it is true that your Core Proposition will resonate powerfully with all of your stakeholders, that doesn't mean it resonates with each group in exactly the same way. For Elevate's "Elevate your credibility," there is a different meaning for the company (enhancing the brand) than there is for an individual at the company sending out a newsletter through Elevate's service (reputation). You can argue that enhancing a company's brand and enhancing a person's reputation are essentially the same thing, which is true, but when Elevate is trying to sell its service to a company, it will tell the story slightly differently than it will when it is trying to sell its service to an individual at the company. The story is essentially the same, but it is nuanced differently.

Brian Bloom, the CEO of Bloom Burton, says, "In any one day, we can be pitching to a start-up, an individual investor, an institutional investor, another investment bank with whom we are partnering, or the media. We now tell the same story to all of them. The first two-thirds of our presentation deck stays the same. The last few slides customize our story to the audience. In the past, we would have ten different decks, and we would then customize one of those decks to the company or audience we were pitching because we didn't have a clear handle on our story. Now it is one deck with a few standardized slides that are different for each audience. Way simpler and way clearer!"

The question "What do I get?" can be expanded to "If you deliver on your Core Proposition for me, what do I get?" If a company has five different key stakeholders, we will usually have five different answers to the question "What do I get?" The answer for each is, typically, two sentences at the most. Once we have an answer for a stakeholder, that statement also answers the question "How do I nuance the story to this particular stakeholder?" As you look to translate the Core Story into a marketing and sales pitch, you look to the answers under the "What do I get?" section to figure out how to tailor the pitch to each stakeholder.

The most important factor in determining the answer to "What do I get?" is its emotional state as it relates to the Core Proposition. The AHRC's Core Proposition is "Building prosperous commercial relationships." Why does it need to do that? Why can't a company and an Aboriginal community not just create a prosperous commercial relationship on its own?

The answer is rooted in trust. Because the cultures of the company and the Aboriginal community it is dealing with are so fundamentally different and foreign to each other, and because Aboriginal communities have been given the short end of the stick for so long, they don't trust companies. They don't feel understood and they don't feel like their broader range of issues (such as ecological and cultural preservation) are respected and addressed in business relationships. When a married couple is dealing with troubles in their relationship, they are often speaking at cross-purposes and, as a result, can't get things resolved.

The same is true in business negotiations between companies and Aboriginal communities. More often than not, the vast difference in cultures has them speaking at cross-purposes. Like a married couple, they need a trusted outsider with a deep understanding of the needs of both parties to create an environment in which they hear each other, respect each other and can come up with a solution that both sides trust.

Since we answer the question "What do I get?" at the end of the Blueprint, by that point we have had many conversations about the Emotional Resonance of the Core Proposition to each stakeholder group (the most important stakeholder being the customer). In chapter 3, we mentioned that we bulletproof that Core Proposition. The way we do that is by determining whether it has a powerful Emotional Resonance with each stakeholder group. If it does, the Core Proposition survives. So by the time we get to the question "What do I get?" it should just be a matter of boiling those discussions down to a statement or two for each key stakeholder.

The two most important stakeholders for the AHRC are Aboriginal communities and companies. Here are the answers to "What do I get?" for each of those stakeholders:

1. **For indigenous peoples:**
   - I trust that the company understands me and respects what is important to me, and as a result will give me a fair deal that I can live with over the long term.
2. **For a company:**
   - I am trusted by the Aboriginal community with whom I am doing the deal, and Aboriginal communities with whom I am negotiating other deals will see that I respect them and can be trusted.

Note here that the Aboriginal statement says they have to feel trust, whereas the company statement says they have to be trusted. The reason the company's statement doesn't also say it has to feel trust is because the Aboriginal community has the majority of the leverage. In an example where a resource company wants to exploit minerals on Aboriginal lands, which is so often the case, the Aboriginal community has to agree in order for the project to go forward. If it is not satisfied with the deal, it will say no. Does this mean that the company doesn't want to come out of the negotiations feeling like it can trust the Aboriginal community? No. It just means it isn't the most important emotional need for the company in trying to forge a business relationship with an Aboriginal community. Being trusted by the Aboriginal community is what will help it achieve its goals.

Longo's Core Proposition is "Treating you like family." Because it's a regional supermarket chain, shopping at its stores or dealing with the company has a very different feel from what you get at its larger competitors, none of them with the history or the culture to credibly pull off a Core Proposition like "Treating you like family." Although it is a regional chain, it is still a big company with big stores. But it has a local grocery store vibe. Let's see how it answers the question "What do I get?" for customers, employees (Longo's refers to them as team members) and suppliers.

1. **As a customer, I trust that you really understand me and that you make me feel important because:**
    - You show, through the quality and assortment of products you offer, that you recognize the role great food plays in my life (personal, family, social, nutritional).
    - Your team members make me feel like they really care about me.
    - You are working hard to have a long-term relationship with me.
    - You wouldn't do anything for me that you wouldn't do for your own family.

2. **As a team member, I have a sense of purpose and pride, and a feeling of belonging because you are committed to:**
    - My personal growth through training and development programs to help me be the best I can be.
    - Recognizing and rewarding me for my role in our shared success.
    - The health and welfare of me and my family through benefits programs.
    - Encouraging, supporting and providing me with opportunities for community involvement.
    - Creating a culture and work environment that feels both physically and emotionally safe.

3. **As a supplier, I have a more rewarding relationship because:**
    - Of how respectfully you treat me through open, honest communication and clear expectations.
    - You give me the opportunity to be innovative and creative, even if you don't always accept what I am offering.
    - You give me the opportunity to prove my long-term value to you, regardless of my size.

- I feel like you are committed to my success in our working relationship.
- You deliver on your commitments.

As a customer, if Longo's treated you like family, how would that make you feel? You would feel respected, understood, cared for and protected. That is exactly how Longo's answered the question "What do I get?" for customers. Note that the answer goes way beyond and way deeper than something as superficial and trans-actional as "a good deal on good products." Longo's is not only committed to creating long-term relationships with its customers, above and beyond the products it offers, but it proves it in how it interacts with its customers on a daily basis. To Longo's, this is more than just a business imperative—a way to sell more. It is a matter of values and pride to the Longo family. When you deal with the executive team and the family, you really get the impression that they would rather shut down the business than not live by the mantra "Treating you like family."

There are not many companies in the world that go to extra-ordinary lengths to make their employees happy and make them feel like they are being treated fairly. Long before its Blueprint, Longo's was an example of the kind of company that under-stood—and, more important, acted upon—the belief that its most important asset is its people. While so many companies pay lip service to this notion, Longo's lives it every day.

Countless studies show that one of the most important things to employees is to feel a sense of purpose and a sense of belonging. They want to feel like they are doing something meaningful and they want to feel like they are part of a community that accepts them, values them and respects them. Creating a culture that is based on a sense of purpose and a sense of belonging is enough in itself to engender long-term, rewarding relationships with employees. In point number two above, Longo's speaks directly to this kind of culture, which is captured in its Core Proposition, "Treating you like family." As an employee, fostering my personal growth, acknowledging my contribution, supporting the health and well-being of my family, encouraging and supporting my contribution to the community, and keeping me safe are all the kinds of things that I would expect from a company that treats me like family.

That Longo's would be committed to its customers and employees is not so surprising. What is surprising is that it is just as committed to the success and well-being of its suppliers. Part of the reason for this is that living the Core Proposition with all of its stakeholders is a point of pride for the Longo family, its management and its team members. But there is also a business imperative for Longo's to treat its suppliers like family: all the big supermarket chains deal with essentially the same suppliers, but that doesn't mean the suppliers treat all of their clients the same. Larger clients will usually get preferential treatment because of their buying power. They will typically get the best pricing, servicing and supply management. They will usually also get a first look at innovative products a supplier develops, which gives them the opportunity to make exclusive deals that lock competitors out.

As a David competing against Goliaths, Longo's doesn't have these advantages. So it has to work hard in other aspects of its relationships with suppliers in order to try to get on an even keel with its larger competitors. As a Longo supplier, having open and honest communication, clearly expressing your expectations of me, fostering my creativity, respecting me and treating me fairly even though I may be small, and delivering on your commitments to me all make me feel like you are dedicated to my long-term success. When a supplier feels that way about a client, more often than not it will go the extra mile for that client, giving it better service than clients who bring in more revenue but don't treat it as well. This is how Longo's works to level the playing field with its larger competitors in its relationships with suppliers.

Emeritus, the wealth management firm, "follows the smart money" on behalf of its clients, using the same investing and draw-down strategies as those who are rich enough to afford their own private teams of dedicated money managers. Unlike most of the other companies we have used as examples, it doesn't have a number of stakeholders to which it is accountable. Its "What do I get?" answers all relate to its customers.

Emeritus's clients are all people who are well off enough that they have hundreds of thousands or even millions of dollars to invest in their retirement. In examining the emotional mindset of these investors, it would be easy to conclude that it all revolves around growing their money. It seems obvious that if you are investing their money, their primary concern would be seeing that money grow at an acceptable rate. But the reality is, for most of these people, their biggest fears are that they don't have enough money to sustain them through their retirement and that, when they invest their money, they will lose it and have to continue to work when they thought they would be travelling.

There is no question that people want to see their money grow, but fear of not having enough for retirement is their biggest concern. So the answer to the question "What do I get?" if I give my business to Emeritus has to speak directly to that fear. And it has to transform that fear into optimism. Here are the answers to "What do I get?" if I am a Emeritus client:

- Relief that I can be in control of my life because I know exactly what I need to do to live the life I want without worrying about running out of money.

- The power to make important life choices confidently and effectively because I have absolute awareness of my financial capability relating to those choices.
- Should conditions change, the ability to adapt intelligently to keep the financial plan for my life on track.

We just want to be clear that, after hearing the Emeritus story, no prospect is going to sit across the table and blurt out, "What a great story! I now feel relief that I can be in control of my life. Sign me up!" What the story does is inspire *feelings* of relief and being in control. The story speaks into the operative feeling—fear—and returns feelings of relief and being in control, all of which exist in your limbic system, the part of your brain that is about feelings and emotions.

We use the word *power* quite deliberately in the second point because when you feel fear, you usually feel powerless. We are not talking about the level of fear that makes adrenaline gush through your body and gives you the strength or power to lift a car to free somebody trapped underneath. We are talking about everyday anxieties of the sort most of us frequently have around money. These are the kinds of fears that diminish us. We feel our options have been narrowed and it is more difficult to make decisions. When the fear is mitigated, our power returns. We feel hopeful and optimistic and confident again. Making decisions, even difficult ones, is easier. This is what we mean by *power*. When the Emeritus story resonates with the client, the client feels hopeful, optimistic and confident, which equals powerful.

If you construct a sales story that just says, "Don't worry because we do A, B, C, D and E to ensure the security of your money," some people might buy it. But unless they are really savvy investors, they won't truly understand what those things are. Meanwhile, every other financial advisor is saying the same thing. This kind of story is a rational argument and speaks into the cerebral cortex, a part of the brain that we know doesn't drive decision making.

"Following the smart money" is a highly complex financial strategy but a very simple story to explain to even the least savvy investor. It goes like this:

- Rich people who can afford their own private team of money managers invest very differently from the way mainstream financial advisors do for their clients.
- They recognize that there are two broad market cycles that last approximately two decades each: one that is constantly rising and one that is essentially flat. Their investment strategy in the first market cycle is entirely different from the one they deploy in the other. Most mainstream financial advisors don't differentiate between these two market cycles; they sell you the same off-the-shelf financial products (like mutual funds), no matter which cycle we are in.
- Your drawdown strategy has to be as sophisticated as your investment strategy because, after you retire, you can lose as much money in the way you take your money out as you made while building your nest egg.

That is the Emeritus elevator pitch. The psychological under-pinnings of the story are rooted in fear, but the story itself never speaks directly to fear. It works on the basis that if fear is the opera-tive emotion around a person's retirement money, "Following the smart money" is the antidote.

"Following the smart money" works as the antidote to fear because of what the rest of us know, or think we know, about rich people. We know that rich people live in big houses, drive fancy cars, have closets full of expensive clothes, go to their cottages on weekends and spend a lot of time travelling around the world. Rich people are obviously doing something right with their money, and we want to do what they're doing so that we can have all the things they have.

All of this information—what we know about rich people—is embedded in our brains already. When you tell people the "Following the smart money" story, you are tapping into their preconceived notions about how effectively rich people manage their money. Those preconceived notions validate the smart money story. In other words, as they listen to the "Following the smart money" story, their preconceived notions about how rich people manage their money serve as proof for them that the story is valid.

6

Business Architecture

To Talk the Talk, You Have to Walk the Walk

Your Core Proposition guides everything that you do and say because it is the articulation of your DNA. As we described in the past, just as your DNA controls virtually all of the development of your body, your corporate DNA controls—or should control—the development of every aspect of the operation of your company or organization. This chapter is about how to use your Core Proposition to align all of the parts of the business—or Business Architecture, as we call it—with who you really are at your core.

When your entire organization is completely aligned with who you are at your core, you have complete clarity about who you are and where you're going. You have greater confidence to lead your company into a bigger future. Your executives will be more creative and innovative. You will see new opportunities for revenue that were never visible to you before. Your people will have a sense of purpose that will inspire them to operate at a higher level. And sales will come faster and easier. We will describe each of these outcomes in more detail in later chapters, but for now, let's look at how you transform your company using your Core Proposition.

You start the process of aligning your Business Architecture with your Core Proposition by asking a simple question: "If I were to make this part of my business truer to my Core Proposition, what would I do?" There are three general answers to this question:

1. Nothing, because this part of my business is already wonderfully aligned with my Core Proposition.
2. I would do the following _____ (fill in the blank). (This chapter deals primarily with this answer.)
3. I would stop doing this because it has nothing to do with my Core Proposition. (Here is a hypothetical example taken to an extreme to make this point: if you are an accounting firm that has a division that rents cars, the car rental division is probably not true to the accounting firm's Core Proposition.)

Aligning Your Business Architecture

Since aligning your Business Architecture with your Core Proposition is usually an exercise of modifying elements of what you currently do, let's look at a few examples of organizations who have gone through this process to make themselves more competitive.

United Van Lines' Business Architecture

In chapter 4, we used the expression "perceived standard of care." As we begin to talk about how the Core Proposition impacts the Business Architecture of a company, that phrase is significant. If a major issue in the moving business is the certainty around the arrival time of the truck, a moving company has two choices to create certainty:

1. Figure out a way to have all trucks arrive on time or earlier 100 per cent of the time. This is impossible!

2. Figure out a way to give customers certainty about the arrival time, even if the actual arrival time is going to be later than promised. This is doable.

We started to explore the ways in which the company could use the guidance of "A higher standard of care" to solve the certainty problem. In other words, what can you do to deliver a higher standard of care around arrival times? One answer is to make sure that all drivers have cell phones so that they can keep clients abreast of their progress. Keep in mind the problem is certainty, not being on time. If somebody gives you advance warning that they will be late, you have certainty. You will have the opportunity to change your plans, if necessary, so that you don't have to sit around twiddling your thumbs while you wait for the truck. You may be a little upset that they are going to be late, but at least you won't be angry and frustrated because you feel like nobody cares. So this is one solution to the problem.

The challenge around this solution is that it requires the company to provide drivers with cell phones, to monitor the cell phone usage so that it isn't abused, to train drivers to have more empathy for the customer—so that they think to call them if they know they're going to be late and to give them periodic updates of their ETA.

In theory, this is a viable solution . . . as long as drivers execute it to perfection. However, there is the risk that, in their preoccupation with getting to their destination safely and on time, drivers will forget to do this. To solve this problem, we asked, "How can we offer an even higher standard of care?" Another option we discussed was having a GPS in every truck so that their exact locations could be tracked on a second-by-second basis. That would provide a means for creating certainty.

But how do you factor customers into the GPS equation so

that *they* can have certainty? You give each customer their own sign-in page on the company website. On their moving day, they can sign in and track the second-by-second progress of their moving truck on Google Maps. They can now see whether the truck is going to be on time, and they will have immediate warning if the truck is having any kind of experience that will delay its arrival. Airlines do this, so it is really just a matter of borrowing a successful practice from them.

The beauty of this system is that it recognizes that it's not being late that bothers people: it is the uncertainty around the arrival time. When people are given advance warning that you are going to be late, they're usually forgiving. It is only when you don't give them advance warning and you're late that they get angry because you created uncertainty. You've attacked their sense of control. Giving your customers the ability to track the progress of the truck on the website gives them the feeling of total control, even though they have virtually no control over the progress of the truck.

The GPS was a tactical solution to an important problem that was guided by the Core Proposition "A higher standard of care"—for customers. The problem we haven't addressed yet is: How does head office provide member companies with a higher standard of care?

If you recall, the initial problem was that head office was creating programs that weren't being used by member companies, and that made members feel like head office didn't care about them. A factor in the creation of this problem was that head office was developing these programs without the input of member companies. Head office would create a program and then try and convince the member companies to use it. Many of them worked, but for those that didn't, the member companies could always immediately see the program's shortcomings.

So if the underlying problem is lack of input from the members, the obvious solution is to elicit input from the members. In the Blueprint sessions, a process was developed that not only solved the problem of creating truly valuable innovations for the member companies but also transformed the culture of the organization from hierarchical to democratic. And it was all guided by a conversation about striving for a higher standard of care.

Head office created a task force system for decision making and problem solving for the company. First, head office identified the 35 most important things that the company had to make decisions on or develop solutions for, and then it created the task force for each. Each task force had its own web page in a members-only area of the company website. Every task force had five to eight members, and any member company could volunteer through the website to be on a task force. Each task force also had somebody from head office and met on a periodic basis by conference call.

The task force infrastructure that head office created enabled member companies to make decisions and develop solutions about the things that were most important to them. Head office didn't have to worry any more about whether or not decisions or solutions were relevant to the members because they were being made *by* the members *for* the members.

But it gets better. Every task force kept minutes of its meetings and posted these to their respective web pages. Any member company could visit any task force's web page and track the progress that group was making in solving its problem. This enabled any member company to have input into the progress of any task force; it could see what was happening, pick up the phone and talk to any task force member to give its point of view. While the task force itself met by conference call, any member company who wasn't on that task force could sit in on the conference call and listen to what was happening. It couldn't participate in the discussion, because coming up with a solution was the job of just the five to eight people on the task force. But any member company could sit in, find out what was going on and then provide its feedback to task force members after the meeting.

This fundamentally changed the way the business operated, and it made member companies feel as if head office was providing them with a higher standard of care. The reward came less than a year later, when this company was named by Deloitte as one of the top 50 privately owned companies and its CEO became the spokesperson that year for the companies in the top 50.

Elevate's Business Architecture

Now let's look at Elevate, the online publishing company whose Core Proposition is "Elevate your credibility." The company was originally named Connected^N. What did Connected^N mean? We didn't know either. It became very clear to everyone involved in its Blueprint that the name Connected^N had nothing to do with who it really was and what it really did: elevate its clients' credibility. To the company's credit, there was no pushback from the founding partners when we challenged the value of the name. Just like us, they could look at the name, look at their Core Proposition and see that one had nothing to do with the other.

It was evident to everyone that the company needed a new name. We suggested that they admit the obvious, that they were about elevating, and just call the company Elevate. They agreed immediately and set out to create its new corporate identity.

We then asked the question "If your promise is to elevate my credibility, how do I know my credibility is being elevated?" The answer was "You don't." So we then explored ways in which the company could actually measure the increase in credibility that the service was providing.

As you publish through an email newsletter, Twitter, LinkedIn,

Facebook and your blog, there are many things that can be tracked. For instance, if you send out an email newsletter, you can track how many people open it and how many people forward it. If people are intrigued enough to open your newsletter, that says something about your credibility. The more people open it, the more credibility you have, especially if that number grows over time. Even better, if they read it and forward it to somebody else because they think it is relevant to that person, that makes a bigger statement about your credibility. On top of *that,* when they forward it to others, they are doing it to elevate their own credibility.

Tracking how many of your email newsletters are opened, and especially how many are forwarded, and how those numbers grow over time is one way to track your increase in credibility. Other ways include how many times you are retweeted or mentioned on Twitter, or how many times you are "liked" on Facebook. There are many other tangible, quantifiable ways you can track how people are responding to what you are publishing.

It was determined in the Blueprint that Elevate could aggregate all of these factors into a single score, called a C-score, that tracks the change in your credibility over time. Even better, a C-score can be tracked for you personally, for your department or for your company as a whole. A C-score serves two important purposes:

- It provides the client with tangible, quantitative evidence that justifies the purchase of the service.
- It inspires loyalty to, and usage of, the service by feeding the egos of individual users, departments and companies because everyone wants to see their C-score go up and nobody wants to see their C-score go down.

The creation of the C-score was by far the most substantial part of Elevate's Business Architecture that had to be modified as a result of its Blueprint. In fact, it wasn't a modification at all; it had to be created from scratch. It was a missing piece of the business that needed to be developed. Developing the C-score was not an insignificant process. As a start-up with limited resources, Elevate had to raise money and hire a more experienced development team to create this complex software element.

As we explained in the Elevate case study, the company's sales story was long, rambling and off-topic. So another part of the Elevate Business Architecture that needed to be modified was its marketing and sales communication. The partners found a clever producer of corporate animations to tell their story and asked us if we would help them prepare a script. This is not our forte by any means, but they are friends now as well as clients and we wanted to do whatever we could to help them grow.

One of the partners started briefing us on what he thought the script should say. We started to recognize a pattern to the points he wanted in the script and realized that they were all contained in one of the answers in the Core Story, which is the third part of the Blueprint and is explained in chapter 5. We reread the Core Story and realized that all we had to do was take one section and make a few modifications to make it more script-like, and it would be ready to record. Within less than half an hour, the script was ready. A few weeks later, the partners returned to show us the animation. We were stunned. It knocked our socks off . . . so much so, we immediately hired that same producer to create a corporate animation for us!

Now, here's the kicker: Elevate's story used to take 45 minutes to tell. This animation told their story—powerfully—in 48 seconds!

Baycrest Hospital's Business Architecture
About nine months after the conclusion of Baycrest's Blueprint, we received an email from the hospital CEO saying they had retained

Deloitte to do their strategic plan, the process was finished, and he would like us to review it and provide comments. After reading through the strategic plan, and before we talked with the CEO of Baycrest, we said to each other that Deloitte's plan was exactly like the Blueprint. We loved what Deloitte had done!

When we met with the CEO, we opened the meeting with the comment that it was interesting that Baycrest had gone through the Blueprint process and ended up in a certain place, and then hired Deloitte independently of that to do a full-blown strategic plan and ended up in the same place. So it seems that each process validated the other. To which the CEO replied, "What are you talking about? I handed Deloitte the Blueprint and said make a strategic plan that follows it." After not hearing from Baycrest for a while and thinking they had forgotten about us, we found out to our pleasant surprise that they had actually been executing on the Blueprint beautifully.

We know our limitations. We are not great at creating the detailed action plan that is the necessary outcome of the Blueprint. Just as a traditional strategic planning process is missing the first part—the clear, concise and compelling identification of who you are—a Blueprint doesn't contain the detailed action plan that answers the question "How will you get there?" By following the direction of the Blueprint, Deloitte had created a very detailed and robust action plan or road map for what Baycrest had to do with its "business" architecture over the next five years in order to be the world leader in innovation in aging as it relates to the brain.

Deluxe Toronto's Business Architecture

Now let's look at some of the ways that Deluxe Toronto had to modify its Business Architecture around innovation using its Core Proposition, "An easier way." As you recall, Deluxe provides services in the field of film and television production.

Leveraging Employees. If you are on a continuous search for an easier way, that means you are in a constant state of innovation. So you want everybody in your company to be constantly innovating. When most companies make this determination, they inform their employees that they want them to be more innovative . . . and then nothing happens. If you're told to be more innovative without any more specific direction than that, you have no guidance for what kind of innovation the company wants, and therefore no incentive to innovate.

One of the initiatives developed in the Deluxe Toronto Blueprint was a competition based on *Dragons' Den* and *Shark Tank,* popular TV shows in which budding entrepreneurs stand in front of a panel of successful businesspeople and pitch their ideas in the hope of getting funding. The Deluxe Toronto version is to have employees, either individually or in groups, conceive of and develop innovative ideas that achieve the goal of finding an easier way for their clients to do their jobs. Employees present their ideas in front of a panel, which gives the idea either a thumbs-up or a thumbs-down. If the verdict is thumbs-up, the employees are given a reward and the support to develop that initiative into a product or service. If it is thumbs-down, the employees are given constructive criticism and encouraged to come back and pitch again in six months.

Market Intelligence. Another way Deluxe Toronto can innovate more effectively is to become more in tune with the constantly evolving needs of its clients. What came out of the Blueprint was a simple initiative with multiple parts that was based on the incredibly obvious idea that if you want to know what your clients need, ask them! Here are some of the modifications Deluxe made in order to glean more information from its clients:

- More contact with clients that isn't sales- or service delivery–related (e.g., lunches)
- Customer advisory board (to meet quarterly to offer suggestions and vet ideas)
- Client round tables for discussions about industry issues
- Stealing good ideas from competitors (why not?)
- Exit interviews with customers who said no

Client Service. Every time Deluxe Toronto introduced a new service, somebody from inside the company obviously ran that service. But that meant an inconvenience for the client, who had to deal with a different person for every service it bought from the company. The Core Proposition "An easier way" made Deluxe realize that this was not an easier way for the client. The company modified its service infrastructure so that it provided each client with a single point of contact. That one person inside Deluxe Toronto managed the delivery of every service the client bought. This was an easier way for the client.

None of these ideas were invented by Deluxe Toronto, but that doesn't matter. As a result of the focus and direction provided by its Core Proposition, "An easier way," Deluxe Toronto was able to make changes to its Business Architecture that served the client better.

Modifying Your Business Architecture

With a careful look, you can see that most companies are modifying their Business Architecture on a daily basis. They're constantly looking for ways to improve and, as a result, are doing anything from tinkering to overhauling every day. The challenge with this process is that it is often like throwing spaghetti at the wall and seeing what sticks. You change and change and change, and some stuff works and other stuff doesn't.

The value of having a clear, concise and compelling answer to the question "Who am I?" as an organization is that you now have a direction in which to change that is true to who you are at your core. As long as the changes are consistent with your Core Proposition, you will have a much higher likelihood of success.

The next five chapters show ways in which a company's Business Architecture can be shifted in order to align with its Core Proposition.

PART 3

After the Pain Comes the Gain

7

Strategic Filter

Distinguishing Right from Wrong

One of the most common clichés about business performance is the need to get everyone in the organization singing from the same songbook. Singing from the same songbook means that everybody in the organization understands who the company is and where it is going, has a common sense of purpose and can consistently make decisions that are aligned with the company's goals.

If you take our Clarity Test at the end of this book, you can get a sense of the levels of effort and commitment that are required by a leadership team to ensure that everybody in the organization is operating in unison. When there are barriers standing in the way of a universal understanding of who the company is and where it's going, it decelerates the pace of the company's growth.

A company's Core Proposition is one of the simplest and most powerful tools *everybody* involved can use to make sure their decisions and actions are aligned with the company's goals. The Core Proposition acts like a strategic filter that guides every decision made and every action taken by every employee and stakeholder. As you can see from the Clarity Test, it isn't enough for the CEO to have a clear vision, or even for the entire management team to be operating in unison. *Everybody* in the organization needs to know how to make decisions that are consistent with who the company is and where it is going. To ask employees to do so without giving them a tangible tool that provides them with guidance on how to do it is a recipe for failure.

We will start out by explaining this idea in a general sense and then will show you how companies have used their Core Propositions to guide their decision making. When you look at a Core Proposition like Bloom Burton's "A faster path to monetization," you can see how all employees can ask themselves, "Is what I'm doing accelerating the path to monetization for this client?" If the answer is yes, they know they are on the right track. If the answer is no, either they need to make some kind of shift themselves or they need to take the problem to others in the organization to help them resolve it.

When we focus on single employees and the implications of a "no" answer, you can see a number of positive benefits for the company and its clients.

> **Battling complacency.** Complacency is one of the most malignant afflictions to infect any company. The expressions "we always do it this way" or "we never do it that way" are recipes for stagnation. If the employee knows that she has to constantly ask herself if what she is doing is consistent with her organization's Core Proposition, she is always questioning whether or not she is doing the right thing for her client. To have all of your employees doing this all of the time creates an organizational culture that is constantly questioning itself, in a constant state of renewal and in a constant state of diligence around ensuring it is doing what is in the best interest of its clients.

Continuous innovation. If you agree with the belief that if you aren't moving forward, you are moving backward, then you must also agree with the need to be in a continuous state of innovation. Innovation is the lifeblood of any company wanting to stay relevant in a rapidly changing world. If the Bloom Burton employee answers "no" to the question "Is what I am doing contributing to a faster path to monetization?" she needs to figure out an alternative approach, whether on her own or in partnership with others in the organization. In other words, without receiving any special skill or training, she and the people with whom she collaborates become innovation engines for Bloom Burton on a daily basis. If the leadership at Bloom Burton were to merely instruct its people to be more innovative, they probably wouldn't know what to do, either, because they would have thought they were already being innovative and wouldn't know what to do differently, or because the instruction was so vague. If, instead, the leadership team tells employees to constantly question whether what they are doing is truly creating a faster path to monetization, they each become innovation engines without even knowing it.

Now let's look at how some of the companies we are following used their Core Propositions to make important strategic or operational decisions.

Bloom Burton & Co.: "What Should Our Corporate Structure Be?"

Armed with its Core Proposition—"A faster path to monetization"—Bloom Burton realized it had some serious structural work it had to do in order to align itself with who it was. It had to simplify and integrate its multiple brands and companies into a single functioning unit with services that led to a faster path to monetization.

It started by shutting down Vancia Group, its management consulting company, and making it a service within Bloom Burton. While it couldn't do the same with its direct investing company for regulatory reasons, the company presents direct investing as one of Bloom Burton's many services.

With its restructuring complete, Bloom Burton was now essentially (if not technically) a single company offering a faster path to monetization by offering clients one or more of five services:

- Public and private capital raising
- Mergers and acquisitions advisory
- Equity research in Canada's health care sector
- Monetization planning (consulting)
- Direct investing

Bloom Burton's Core Proposition became the decision-making filter that drove it to develop a simpler structure with a simpler, more compelling story. When it realized it was in the business of "A faster path to monetization," it became self-evident that its services worked together in an integrated way to help companies reach their monetization goals. Each service had to appear to be a piece of the puzzle, working in harmony with both how the company was structured and how the story was told.

Eckler: "How Do We Determine Which Clients Are Right for Us?"

A common mistake for many companies is to take on business that doesn't end up being profitable. When you have a new business opportunity, how do you decide if it's right for you? The primary decision-making tool Eckler uses is its Core Proposition.

A large pension plan was looking to replace its pension computer system by purchasing one from suppliers who operated in a highly commoditized market. While this was a project that Eckler had the capability to take on, the question was: Is this the kind of business that was right for Eckler's future, and would it be profitable? Remember, a Core Proposition applies to all stakeholders, not just customers. "A greater degree of certainty" applies to Eckler's decision-making process just as much as it applies to what it delivers to its clients.

Therefore, Eckler had to feel "A greater degree of certainty" in the decisions it made. Replacing a pension computer system that did not require tailored customization did not meet the standard for Eckler. Although pension systems development is part of its core business, its focus is on developing highly customized tailored solutions for its clients. This project was better suited to the many other companies that simply sell their off-the-shelf systems less expensively. Eckler debated whether or not it was worthwhile to drop its price on this project in order to get the business, hoping that the new relationship with this company would lead to downstream business that would be profitable. In other words, it would have to lose a significant amount of money on this project in order to earn money later in the relationship. Another way to look at it is that Eckler would have to invest its own money in this project in order to do it properly.

This is a common dilemma that many companies face: Do we take business at a loss now in order to create a relationship with the client that will result in revenue later? There is no blanket correct answer; you have to take it on a case-by-case basis. Eckler had to answer two questions in order to determine whether or not this was a worthwhile investment:

1. How real was the possibility of getting downstream business from this new client?
2. If Eckler was able to get downstream business, how much would it be worth, and would it be profitable?

There was no way for Eckler to answer these questions with any degree of certainty, let alone a greater degree of certainty. After much debate, during which the company tried to answer these questions with a greater degree of certainty—and couldn't—it decided to pass on this business opportunity. What cemented the decision was that there was too much potential for business elsewhere that did offer them a greater degree of certainty for them to spend their time on a speculative opportunity that required a significant investment of money for an uncertain return.

Longo's: "Do We Actively Promote an Employee Benefit That Is Going to Cost Us a Lot of Money?"

"We have a retirement savings program in which we match every dollar an employee puts in," says Anthony Longo, Longo's CEO. "But we had only a 37 per cent participation rate—which is crazy, considering that we do matching funds. This is a very generous program that should have 100 per cent enrolment!"

There was a lot of conversation around the executive table about what to do, if anything, about this problem. Financially, it was in Longo's best interest to have a low enrolment rate because it cost the company less money. In the end, what drove the decision to promote the program aggressively to employees was Longo's Core Proposition, "Treating you like family." If these people were truly family members, you would want them to enrol in the program to protect their futures. You wouldn't want them to be financially vulnerable as they grew old; you would want them to have as big a retirement fund as they could possibly afford.

Longo's decided to aggressively promote the retirement plan to its employees in spite of the fact that it would be a large expense. As well as the money the company would have to budget to match funds, there was also the cost of the promotional initiative to make sure that all employees knew about the program, its value to them and how to enrol. Management started a lunch-and-learn campaign, going into the stores and promoting the program to all employees. "This is what you would do for your family," says Anthony Longo. "When people feel cared for, when they feel like they are important to an organization, they will be more loyal, be less likely to leave the company and work harder. In strictly business terms, although it costs us more up front, it costs us less in the long term because our people work harder to help the company grow, and it is cheaper to retain people than to hire new employees when they leave. We get these business benefits because it is core to our values to treat everyone like family."

Momentum: "Is the Company Name Right?"

When we were first introduced to Drew McDougall and his unique condo idea, his company was called Eldergarten. We immediately knew this name had to go! Of course, having just met him, we didn't know his company's Core Proposition, but we had an intuitive sense of what it was and how the name definitely didn't fit with the quality and sophistication of the idea.

To his credit, when we told McDougall that the name was wrong, he said he was open to a name change. The company was young enough that there would be no serious objection in the marketplace to a new name, as long it as it was right. While we appreciated McDougall's open-mindedness, we also knew that founders of start-ups get married to the names they give their companies. They are so invested in the name, it is very emotionally wrenching to give it up.

The original name of the company, Eldergarten, has a strong connotation of old and somewhat dependent. The name is obviously a play on kindergarten, except at the opposite end of the age spectrum. A kindergarten is where dependent children go to play and learn when they are too young to go to school. The name

Eldergarten implied that its customers were old and dependent and needed others who were looking after them. It's a name that would immediately turn off people who still considered themselves to be young and vital and just entering a new phase of life.

It is a testament to the power of words—and the importance of getting them right—that Eldergarten would turn off people who might otherwise like living in one of McDougall's condos. In other words, McDougall risked losing sales to people who might otherwise love his condos just because of the name. If you are in your 50s or 60s, at the peak of your career, and are trading your home for a condo, would you investigate one called Eldergarten? Would you be embarrassed if your friends knew you were living in a building called Eldergarten? For most people who are downsizing, the answers to these questions are no and yes, respectively.

The question became: If not Eldergarten, then what? While we considered lots of options, the name that kept coming to the fore was Momentum. People who are downsizing have focused most of their adult lives on their families and their careers. Because their children have all moved away and they are more or less independent, these people are now able to focus more on themselves. They have the time and the financial wherewithal to invest in themselves—to indulge in the things they have denied themselves while they were serving others. They could buy a cottage, travel more or contemplate a new career. They are entering a stage in their lives that is all about them.

It is almost as if their lives are gaining momentum. They are able to do more of the things they really want to do, without worrying about factoring in careers or dependent children. They have more disposable income and less responsibility. They have crested that first, highest peak on the roller coaster, and now they are ready to experience the speed and thrills that lie ahead of them as they whoosh through the rest of the ride.

This is how McDougall chose Momentum as the name for his company. Unlike Eldergarten, there wasn't an old-age implication to this name. If anything, it was the opposite. To live with momentum, you had to be young—at least at heart—and vital. This is exactly how potential buyers saw themselves, so Momentum, unlike Eldergarten, spoke both to where they are in their lives and what they aspire to be in the future.

Arriving at the name Momentum was a chain reaction that started with characterizing potential condo buyers as downsizers, which led to the Core Proposition "Catering to downsizers' most essential needs," which in turn made us really focus on the emotional mindset of downsizers to determine and validate the name. Without the focus of the Core Proposition, figuring out a proper name would be hit and miss. Without a clear focus, the first run at a name (Eldergarten) was a miss. With a clear focus, Momentum was a hit.

Longo's: "How Do We Make Employees More Accountable to Customers?"

"'Treating you like family' guides our decision making at every level of business," Anthony Longo says. "For instance, we've integrated it into our training program so that our employees are very clear on the standard we expect from them. We use storytelling in our training, using case studies of employees who treated customers like family and examples where this was lacking so that we could really drive home and refine what we meant by 'Treating you like family.'"

"An important aspect of training is accountability; we have to acknowledge what our employees do well and discourage what they do poorly. We had a situation in which a customer had left a number of messages for a store manager, but they all went unreturned. If we didn't know our Core Proposition, we likely would've had a conversation with the manager about how not returning phone calls is not the 'Longo's way.' But what does the 'Longo's way' mean to the store manager? Before we had our Core Proposition, I didn't even know what it meant to me! I had an intuitive sense of what it meant, as did the manager, but we didn't have a common understanding of it throughout the company. The conversation we actually had with the manager was about how he would never let a family member's message go unreturned for days, and, just like family, we have to extend the same level of respect to our customers." This was a much more tangible and beneficial conversation to have with the manager, using common language and a common understanding of the underlying ethos that is meant to drive employee behaviour.

8

Business Confidence/Sense of Purpose

Regaining Your Swagger

We have a CEO as a client who is extremely confident and has earned the right to be so. Both he and his company have a long track record of accomplishment on behalf of their clients. This is no mean feat for this company, because it helps clients in the most intractable of situations. Hence, his Core Proposition: "When you can't afford to lose."

He has given us much good advice over the years, including an appreciation for the role of a Blueprint in building both individual and corporate confidence. At a breakfast we were having with him, he said, "Guys, you have to get that the Blueprint gave me a confidence to talk about and lead my company in a bolder way. I knew we did good work, but being able to capture what we do so succinctly and powerfully gave me more confidence."

We were surprised to hear this from him, because he was already so confident and had achieved so much. He had told us this before, but it hadn't sunk in. Now we finally got it and started asking other clients if it was true for them as well. This is how confidence became one of the major benefits of knowing your Core

Proposition, being able to articulate its underlying story and having a clear, concise and compelling answer to the question "Why should I choose you?"

To understand how your Core Proposition boosts both individual and institutional confidence, we need to understand that there is a disconnect between what many companies do and how they talk about what they do. How many times have you encountered a company that does great work, but when you look at its website or its other marketing materials, or you sit through its new business pitch, you are shocked by how banal it sounds?

This isn't just a marketing and sales problem; it causes a confidence problem as well. As a member of this organization, at whatever level you are at, you are constantly hearing the story of who you are. If that story is boring, it has a negative impact on you emotionally. Why? Because you are human. When you hear the boring story, your reaction is, "But we are so much more than that!" And you are right; you *are*. The problem is that neither you nor anyone else in the organization can articulate the magic of what you do. Emotionally, this is debilitating.

On the other hand, when your company's story captures the full magic of what you do, it has an emotional impact on you as well. It instills in you a sense of pride and confidence. Your reaction is more likely to be "Yes, that's who we are and what we do! Isn't it amazing?"

The CEO we mentioned a few paragraphs ago, by the nature of his work, has set a very high bar for himself and his employees. Clearing that bar as consistently as they do gives them a great deal of confidence. Being able to articulate what they accomplish for their clients in a clear, concise and compelling way nudges up that confidence level even more. Or, as our client said, "It has given us a swagger that is important to how we operate."

But there is more to the swagger than just confidence. It seems like common sense to say that if your employees have a sense of purpose, they will perform better. When you feel like you are a part of a cause, working to a higher purpose, you are more motivated and will contribute at a higher level. This point can be hard to prove because it seems so ethereal, intangible.

Deloitte has been working hard to put some meat on this bone with its annual Core Beliefs & Culture survey. The 2014 edition of this survey has some pretty striking statistics that support the idea that, when employees feel a sense of purpose, their companies perform better. Here is a sampling of some of the insights in the Deloitte study:

	I feel a strong sense of purpose	I don't feel a strong sense of purpose
My organization recorded positive growth last year	81%	67%
I am confident we will record positive growth next year	82%	42%
We will maintain or strengthen our brand reputation and loyalty	91%	49%
My organization will stay ahead of industry disruptions	83%	42%
My organization will remain (or become) the leader in its industry	80%	48%
My organization will outperform the competition	79%	47%
Our clients have long-lasting relationships with us	92%	69%
Our stakeholders trust our organization's leadership	81%	54%
Our employees are fully engaged with the organization	73%	23%

These are some pretty striking numbers! If you look only at the last statement—"Our employees are fully engaged with the organization"—the difference between the numbers is pretty frightening. Only 23 per cent of people who work for an organization that doesn't have a sense of purpose feel like its workforce is fully engaged. How scary is that if you are the leader of one of those companies? For sure, there is a financial cost when a workforce is not fully engaged. This is a hidden, and very real, expense on the balance sheet.

In our experience, we've seen precious few companies in which employees truly feel a sense of purpose. This is not to say that people don't enjoy their jobs. But enjoying your job is not the same as having a sense of purpose. Having a sense of purpose raises enjoying your job to a whole new level.

Let's look at Eckler as an example of the distinction between enjoying your job and having a sense of purpose. You have to have a special passion for math to become an actuary. If you choose to study actuarial science in university, you know you are in for a rough ride. You don't go into this program unless you are fully committed to this life. It is an extremely rigorous program. Dedicating yourself to long hours of study isn't enough. To be a successful actuary, it is almost as if you have to be wired at birth for this discipline. It was very evident from our work with the people at Eckler that they were passionate about math and what it could do. It was also clear that they enjoyed their work.

Eckler's Blueprint was received enthusiastically when it was presented to employees. The Core Proposition, "A greater degree of certainty," and its explanation shifted their perceptions of the company and its prospects for the future in two ways:

- Everybody at Eckler knew that defined-benefit pensions were a declining market. The new direction the company was embarking on—as determined by its Core Proposition—gave them confidence that the company was going to thrive in the future.
- In one of those "be careful what you wish for" moments, many employees started asking to work on the new kinds of

> business that Eckler was going to pursue. Having worked on
> defined-benefit pension problems for so long, employees saw
> the new projects as sexy.

Eckler employees started printing out the Core Proposition and posting it in their cubicles. "A greater degree of certainty" elevated their passion to a cause, giving them a sense of purpose. While we used to view this sense of purpose as an intangible, as we noted above, the Deloitte survey suggests that if your employees don't have a sense of purpose, it is a substantial barrier to growth.

Eckler's Core Proposition is an example of how powerful language can be in changing how we think and feel. We were sitting in front of a board of directors one day, pitching for their business. The chair of the board asked us what intrigued us about them as a client. "Is it that you can go out and pitch other businesses like ours if you are successful with us?" he asked. We were taken aback by the question. "No," we replied. "It's how we change people. It's how fundamentally they think differently about their businesses. That's what we love." Needless to say, we feel a strong sense of purpose and what we do.

VHA: "How Do We Empower Our People to Provide a More Customized Service to Our Clients?"

VHA Home HealthCare sends personal support workers (PSWs) out into people's homes to look after them while they are recuperating. In order to give these clients the best service, it is imperative that these PSWs feel a sense of purpose.

As we have mentioned, your Core Proposition has to resonate with—and apply to—all stakeholders, not just customers. As such, "More independence" must apply to VHA's employees as much as it does to the people it serves.

Personal support workers are the front line for VHA. They are the people who go into the homes of those who are elderly, sick and injured to provide a variety of support services. Every time they visit a client, they do so with a service plan provided by head office. While the service plan is well thought through, the client may have needs that are beyond the scope of that particular visit. This is easy to assess by the PSW, either through observation or through a conversation with the client.

PSWs didn't have the authority to shift the service plans spontaneously. They either had to phone head office and get permission to shift the plan or file a report after the visit so that the plan could be shifted for the next visit. Since most PSWs either didn't have cell phones or didn't get compensated for business calls they made with their personal cell phones, they had to ask clients to use their phones to call head office. Too often, PSWs felt uncomfortable asking clients to borrow their phones, so the service changes had to wait until the next visit.

VHA realized that to serve clients better and stay true to "More independence," it had to provide its PSWs with more independence. The simplest solution was to provide PSWs with mobile devices so they could communicate with head office on an as-needed basis without having to ask clients to use their phones. PSWs were also able to access client files and schedules from their devices and record client preferences in the moment so that all staff had the same up-to-date information on a specific patient.

Being able to change service plans and access client files while they were actually in the client's home empowered PSWs to provide better service to the client. It also engaged PSWs more fully in the planning, modification and execution of service plans. Since they are the ones with the most intimate understanding of the clients' needs at any given moment, it only makes sense to have them more involved in what it takes to serve clients better. This includes a "client preference" note function that allows PSWs to input information about what is typically most important to a specific client—be it a glass of warm milk before bed, a bath at the start of the visit or a brief walk in the hallway to get out and about. PSWs have enthusiastically embraced this function of the technology, which has helped all VHA staff better understand the priorities of its clients.

VHA also created the Simple Comforts Fund, which allows all its care providers, including PSWs, to spend up to $100 without prior approval for something a client needs. If a PSW determines that a client will become more mobile—more independent—with a cane, the Simple Comforts Fund empowers them to just go out and buy a cane for the client and be reimbursed for the purchase.

These two initiatives—providing PSWs with cell phones and the ability to use the Simple Comforts Fund—empowered PSWs in a way they never were before. It gave them a greater involvement in, and sense of ownership over, the well-being of their clients. It sent a message to them that their opinions and expertise were valued. This gave them a greater sense of purpose, which enabled them to contribute at a higher level. When employees feel valued, they work harder and smarter. Both VHA and its clients benefited from the greater contributions PSWs were able to make.

Longo's: "How Do We Give Our Employees a Greater Sense of Ownership over Our Community Giving Program?"

Longo's desire to treat people like family was not something that came from its Blueprint. It came from the three brothers who founded the company decades ago and was passed down through the generations through strong family bonds. So Longo's has been treating people like family for as long as the company has existed. Given that, it is not surprising that the family has a generous program for giving back to the community, both corporately and through a family foundation.

"Our Core Proposition gave greater depth and meaning to our community-giving program," says Anthony Longo. "Because of the expression 'treating you like family,' we were better able to explain to people inside and outside the company why we do what we do in community giving. People who live in our communities who are disadvantaged need our help, so we treat them like family. This is why we do more than just writing cheques. We can have a greater impact on our communities by actually participating in events that help make them stronger.

"Our Core Proposition makes our [community-giving] program tangible, grounding [it] in reality. Our employees get both how and why they need to take an active role in building our communities and helping the disadvantaged."

IQMH: How Do I Embed Confidence and a Sense of Purpose in Our Culture?

"I have never lacked confidence in the quality and importance of IQMH's work," says Dr. Greg Flynn, IQMH's CEO. "I knew at an intuitive level that we delivered incredible value to the health care system, patients, doctors and the people of Ontario, but our Blueprint gave my staff a sense of confidence like mine. They all bought into our Core Proposition, 'Elevating confidence in the system,' and that galvanized them around a higher purpose and gave them a clear idea of where we are going. They now know not only what they are doing, they know why they are doing it.

"This has been transformative for the organization because it institutionalized our purpose. Rather than looking to me as the leader for a sense of purpose, it has become a part of our culture that transcends me and will live in the DNA of the organization long after I am gone. We have an excellent executive team, but strong leadership can take you only so far. Confidence and a sense of purpose has to be the main driver of organizational and individual behaviour."

As one example of that confidence, Dr. Flynn charged his staff with coming up with a name for the organization that was consistent with its Core Proposition. Prior to the Blueprint, there would have been no basis for coming up with the name. Although the organization was clear on the services it provided, there are hundreds or even thousands of names that would have been appropriately descriptive. "In the past, if I had asked them to come up with a new name, they would've come up with a new name because that is what I asked," says Dr. Flynn. "But they surprised me by coming back and recommending we keep the same name because it was consistent with our Core Proposition. They used the Core Proposition to rationalize why the existing name was appropriate, and I agreed. So we are still IQMH (Institute for Quality Management in Healthcare)!"

Eckler: "Do We Make This Substantial Investment?"

Eckler spotted a hole in the market that looked like it could be a good business opportunity. But was it? It would require a significant investment of time, resources and money in order to exploit, so determining its true upside potential was critical to the go-or-no-go decision.

Mortality tables predict life expectancy based on a variety of complex factors. Accurate mortality tables are an essential element in determining many things in the financial world, including pension plan liabilities and insurance rates. The industry-standard mortality tables that are typically used by pension plans were deemed by actuaries and pension plan sponsors not to be accurate enough. This was the hole in the market that Eckler saw. The most basic question it had to answer was "Does it make sense from a financial and resource basis to develop our own mortality tables?"

There were three additional questions it had to answer in order to make this decision:

1. How would it finance the project?
2. Where would it get the necessary baseline data?
3. Would there be a large enough market for the mortality tables that it could derive enough revenue to make the project profitable?

To answer these questions, Eckler went to potential customers and asked them whether they would use more accurate mortality tables, whether they would provide Eckler with the necessary baseline data and whether they would be willing to be partners in the project by providing funding. The answer to all three questions was yes. This provided Eckler with the greater degree of certainty it needed to green-light this project.

Momentum: "How Do I Tell One Story That Captivates Everyone?"

"While downsizers are our target group for the condos," says Drew McDougall of Momentum, "we have ten different stakeholder groups that we have to address. We would tell ten different stories, customized to each of the stakeholder groups, which was a problem in itself, but each of the principals in the company had their own ten different stories. This created a lot of confusion around the nature and value of the communities we were trying to create."

When he first started the company, McDougall wrote ten different white papers, one for each stakeholder group. He tried to reduce it to two, but as he says, "The more we edited these white papers, the less confident we got that we were communicating effectively, that the value of what we were doing was getting through." Using his Core Proposition and his Core Story as his guide, he was able to write one white paper that resonated with stakeholders.

"Now when I send an information package," says McDougall, "I have ten different cover letters, each one customized to a different stakeholder group. But I send only one white paper. I keep getting feedback that the white paper spoke directly to them, even though it wasn't customized for them. We finally had confidence that we could tell one story that captured the full value of what we were doing and know that it was going to captivate the right people."

Bloom Burton & Co.: "How Do We Overcome Founders' Syndrome?"

Here is an aspect of confidence-building that many founders of the company wouldn't have the confidence to admit: the company's mantra, "A faster path to monetization," empowers employees to challenge the leaders when it comes to decision making. "All of our employees know our Blueprint as well as we do," says Brian Bloom. "They know who we are and where we are going, so they have more say in what we do and what we don't do. They support our thinking and our decisions when they are aligned with 'a faster path to monetization,' and they challenge us vigorously when they don't think what we are proposing is aligned. Everyone is accountable to 'a faster path to monetization,' including Jolyon [Burton] and me, and when we can't validate our ideas as being aligned with our Core Proposition, they stand up to us."

"We were introducing a new service, and the senior leadership team was having a conversation about pricing," says Burton. "Brian and I wanted to discount the service to kick-start its introduction. The other members of the leadership team were confident in its value and argued against discounting. I think in many organizations, executives would be uncomfortable challenging the president and the CEO as they did, especially when they are also the owners of the company, but they stood their ground and won the argument. The first client who bought the service paid full price without objection. Brian and I were fortunate that our executive team had so much confidence in the value [of the service] that they stood up to us. When you start out offering something at a discount, it is difficult to raise the price. Their confidence saved us from leaving money on the table."

"Part of their argument for not discounting was that if the client doesn't see the value in the service at its full price, this is not a client that we want to have," says Bloom. "We were confident in the value of the service and confident enough to walk away from the client if they didn't want to buy it at full price."

VHA: "How Do We Give All of Our Employees a Greater Sense of the Value We Provide to Our Clients?"

As we have mentioned, once we arrive at what we think is the Core Proposition, we have to bulletproof it to make sure it resonates with all stakeholders. Two of VHA's most important stakeholders are its employees and the government, which provides most of its funding. So it was on these two stakeholder groups that we focused our bulletproofing process once we realized that "More independence" resonated so effectively with VHA's clients.

While VHA did not have a "command-and-control" culture by any means, it did operate under a traditional hierarchical structure with its personal support workers (PSWs) providing services on the front lines. Simply put, they would get instructions from head office as to what services they were to provide to a client, and then they would go to the client's home and provide those services. The PSW would then report back to the office on what had been done and the current status of the client. This report would help VHA determine the future services the client needed.

What the senior leadership team realized from our conversation is that providing its workforce with more independence would increase the quality of service the clients received and would likely lead to a faster path to providing clients with more independence. While workers were given instructions from head office on what to do with the client, when they got to the client's home, they would often realize that the client needed something different. But PSWs didn't have the authority to change the client plan; if they wanted to change it on the spot, they had to phone head office to get permission. This was a cumbersome process that VHA realized was in nobody's best interest. Giving PSWs the authority and tools to change the treatment plan dynamically would serve the client better and would give PSWs a greater sense of purpose because they would now have the autonomy to make better decisions for the client. So granting PSWs "More independence" resonated with them as much as it did for clients.

We next explored whether or not "More independence" would resonate with VHA's primary funder, the Ontario Ministry of Health and Long-Term Care. With health care expenses that are increasing dramatically every year, the ministry is under constant pressure to control costs. The biggest cost in the health care system is the management of an aging population. The more people can be kept out of expensive institutions as they grow older, the less expensive it is for the health care system to care for them. By helping to keep seniors in their homes, VHA is a valuable ally to the government in keeping costs down. On top of that, if VHA can actually increase the independence of seniors living at home, it will save the government even more money. So it was obvious to us that "More independence" would resonate with the Ministry of Health and Long-Term Care.

"Getting to 'More independence' gave us a rallying cry that allowed us to stand up and say, 'We have value and here's what it is,'" says Carol Annett, CEO of VHA. "It gave us the confidence to state who we are and know that this would resonate with all of our stakeholders, especially our clients, our employees and our government funders. It also allowed us to celebrate our successes more because it gave us a context for what is and isn't success."

"I recognize that our culture was too much 'watch Greg and see what he does,' and not enough about taking initiative," says Greg Flynn, IQMH's CEO. "We were in the process of organizing an international symposium on personalized medicine [genetic medicine to customize treatment for patients]. The planning started before our Blueprint and was progressing in the 'same old, same old' way. After the Blueprint, the organizational staff took more control and initiative and created an excellent format for the symposium. It energized the people who were running it.

"It was a huge success with many international attendees. The symposium was sold out and all of the fee-paying exhibitors were very happy with the quality of the attendees. The impact of the events was recognized by *Dark Daily*, a very influential industry blog. Next year we will have a bigger room and a bigger audience. The organizers had a tremendous sense of pride in taking a risk and having it work. They have the confidence to set more ambitious goals for the future and to stretch themselves to reach those goals."

9

Creativity and Innovation

Transforming Every Employee into an Innovation Engine

Interiors, the retail shelving company whose Core Proposition is "Opening sooner," has staff who serve one of two functions: managing the process of construction, and installing the shelving. On the surface, there doesn't seem to be much need for individual or institutional creativity. In its Blueprint, Interiors asked us what happens if its competitors start copying what it does to get their clients open sooner. The answer is quite simple: just keep looking for new ways to get your clients open even sooner, and you will constantly stay one step ahead of your competition.

For too many companies, innovation is an ad hoc or undirected process. It is often like throwing spaghetti against the wall and seeing what sticks. Most of the spaghetti falls to the floor. This lack of focus decreases the likelihood that you will come up with innovations that are relevant to what you do and that are valuable to clients. This makes the process of innovation slow and expensive.

Innovation is the result of creativity. It is people's creativity, their ability to do imaginative problem solving, that produces innovation. So how do you encourage creativity and give it a disciplined focus when most of your employees are not, by their nature, creative? The good news is that most of your employees are more creative than they may think. Ordinary people are constantly facing obstacles and having to figure out ways to get around them. What you have to do is harness that creativity and focus how it is applied.

Your Core Proposition is the device that both inspires and focuses creativity. As we described in chapter 7, the first step is to train your staff to constantly ask the question "Is what I am doing aligned with our Core Proposition?" If the answer is no, they need to be encouraged to find a better way of doing what they're doing. Maybe they will come up with the innovation themselves, or maybe they will have to collaborate with others. Either way, by asking and answering this question, every one of your employees becomes an innovation engine in the company.

You will be surprised at how quickly people start innovating when they know your Core Proposition. With Interiors, its employees started innovating right from their first exposure to the Blueprint. John Panigas, Interiors' CEO, presented the Blueprint to all of his employees. When he opened up the floor for questions, the first person to speak was a 22-year-old carpenter sitting in the back of the room. He put up his hand and said, "If we are going to be about opening sooner, there should be a space on our weekly time cards where each of us has to write in a suggestion every week for a new way to get finished faster."

You could dismiss this as a "been there, done that" idea, but that would be missing a couple of remarkable points:

1. The first thing that came to his mind upon seeing the Blueprint was an innovative idea for this company. He didn't ask for more explanation of the Blueprint. He didn't complain that it might cause more work. He came up with an idea that was triggered by the Core Proposition, "Opening sooner."

2. While the idea he came up with wasn't unique—many companies do this—it is an innovation that will return many more innovations. As the company sifts through and prioritizes the ideas that are submitted every week, it should be able to find some gold nuggets on an ongoing basis.

Another person who spoke up in that presentation was the company receptionist. All requests for proposals (RFPs) flow through her, and all of them are submitted on the last minute of the last day because that's just how everybody does RFPs. She said that from now on she was going to count back three days from the RFP deadline, and that was going to become the new deadline for Interiors' RFPs. As she explained it, even something as mundane as submitting an RFP should send a signal to prospects that Interiors is about getting finished faster.

What follows are examples of how a Core Proposition triggers creativity within companies, leading to innovation.

Eckler: "How Do We Inject More Creativity into Our Solutions?"

"A greater degree of certainty also guides us in how we provide services for our clients," says Jill Wagman, the firm's managing principal. "It provides both a focus and a scorecard for what we are delivering to each client. When we are designing a program for a client, the ultimate objective is always to provide them with a greater degree of certainty in whatever business problem they are trying to solve. Once we have developed a proposal, and before it goes to the client, we have to justify to ourselves how this creates a greater degree of certainty for them."

Eckler had a client that provides benefit programs to not-for-profit organizations. The client itself was a not-for-profit, so one of the ways it was able to provide cost-effective benefits for its not-for-profit clients was to keep its margins low (in fact, its margins just covered its operating costs). As a not-for-profit itself, Eckler's client didn't have owners or shareholders clamouring for it to return an ever-increasing profit each quarter. Each of the organization's clients went into a common pool so that they all shared both the benefits and the risks.

The risk associated with this model is that you could bring in a new client that is a bad risk for whatever reason. If one client is a bad risk, it could compromise the pool and raise the cost of benefits for all of the other clients that are members of the pool. Because the benefit provider is operating on slim margins, it doesn't have the financial reserves to prop up a pool that is compromised by a single bad-risk member. So it was critical that Eckler's client be able to evaluate whether or not a potential new member was a bad risk. Another way to look at it is: How do you create a greater degree of certainty that a new prospect is a good risk to bring into the pool? In the past, they had always operated on instinct, but they had lost confidence in instinct as a means of making this determination.

"We had to create a greater degree of certainty around who is and isn't a good customer for this client," says Wagman. "We collected massive amounts of historical claims data, built a predictive model based on that data, and from the model identified the criteria for a good customer. We then used those criteria to create a scorecard to evaluate prospects. All our client had to do was look at the score. If the number was high enough, it was a good customer. Too low and they get rejected." The robustness of this new model of evaluation gave Eckler's client more confidence—a greater degree of certainty—in choosing whom to take on as a customer.

VHA: "How Do We Make Our Services More Customized and Relevant?"

When we think of innovation in the business world, we often think of big advances such as the introduction of the iPad, gene sequencing and supercomputing. But as VHA points out in one of its newsletters, it is often the little things, which seem to be insignificant at first glance, that can actually have incredible impact.

One such example was a trial project called Changing the Conversation—co-led by VHA and the Toronto Central Community Care Access Centre—that shifted the emphasis of home care visits by PSWs from "tasks first" to "talk first." This project had two goals: to make home care visits more relevant to clients by listening to their needs—giving them a voice—and to help make them more independent. Instead of arriving at home and working through a checklist of tasks, the first thing PSWs did during the visit was ask three simple questions:

1. What is the most important thing I can help you with today (asked at the beginning of the shift)?
2. I will be leaving in a few minutes. Is there anything else I can help you with before I go (asked at the end of the shift)?
3. Is there anything you would like me to tell the office or the supervisor (asked at the end of the shift)?

PSWs greeted this initiative with mixed feelings. There was a concern that asking these open-ended questions would result in time-consuming requests for tasks that were not relevant to the PSW's work. In other words, would PSWs be asked to do things outside of the scope of their job, like ironing, banking, big grocery trips and large-scale cleaning? There was also excitement about the initiative because it shifted the focus from ticking off all of the tasks on the care plan to-do list to helping clients and their families with the tasks they perceived as most important and most likely to increase independence.

When asked the first question, most clients requested the usual mix of services and personal care tasks. Very few "out of scope" requests were made. On the surface, you might conclude that this question is a waste of time because the client almost always asked for things that the PSW was providing anyway. But the value of this question was not just in the specifics of the answer; it was also in the fact that the client played a role in their own care and felt heard. How does this contribute to "More independence"? When a client feels heard, they feel empowered. They feel more in control of their lives and their care program. They *feel* more independent, and that is an important psychological factor in the quality of their lives.

When asked, "Is there anything I can help you with before I go?" almost half of the clients were entirely satisfied with services provided during the visit and didn't want anything more. Those who did want extra help requested comfort or assistance that could easily be provided in the time remaining. These were requests for food or drink, moving to a new location of the home or small housekeeping tasks.

These questions drove a remarkable shift in clients' and families' overall satisfaction with their personal support service. On a scale of one to ten, the average client rating of personal support service in the pilot project was 9.3, compared to 7.4 for clients not participating. Even when clients didn't need or want any additional service, they appreciated being asked, being given some choice about how they received care and having the flexibility to set their own priorities. The success of the initiative was such that it is being expanded to reach across all populations and services.

This initiative had a big impact on PSWs as well. The fear that there would be requests that were out of scope proved to be unfounded. With no downside to the program, PSWs felt more engaged in the process with their clients because they were actually playing a role in the planning and execution of their care. They weren't just going in and doing all of the to-do's on their checklist; they were listening to their clients and providing them with what they really needed in order to make their visits productive. The Changing the Conversation initiative gave PSWs more independence in how they serve their clients, and that gives them a greater sense of purpose.

Baycrest: "How Do We Embed Innovation into the Culture?"

"I had to figure out how to further embed innovation into the organization," says Dr. Bill Reichman, CEO. "We couldn't just maintain the status quo. We had to create an innovation engine inside the organization in order to be true to who we are and who we aspired to be in the future." Using "Innovation in aging" as the context for its proposal, Baycrest applied for and received a $10 million grant from the government to create the Centre for Brain Fitness.

"We wanted to create an innovation lab inside the Centre for Brain Fitness, but we weren't sure how to do that," says Reichman. "So we went to other institutions around the world that had innovation labs to learn what made them successful. We selected the best elements of what they were doing and the ones that fit with our assets and capabilities and designed our own model. We created the Innovation Technology and Design Lab (ITDL) at the heart of the Centre for Brain Fitness.

"An important influence on the ITDL was an article I read in *The New Yorker* on Nathan Myhrvold, a former senior executive at Microsoft. One of the things Myhrvold pursued after he left Microsoft was his passion for paleontology. He wondered why it took so long to find Tyrannosaurus rex bones when there were so many of them scattered all over the Earth. He wanted to figure out how to accelerate the process of finding Tyrannosaurus rex bones, so he assembled a multidisciplinary team of experts, not just paleontologists, to work together to try to solve the problem."

> From The New Yorker: "Our expeditions have found more T. rex than anyone else in the world," Myhrvold said. "From 1909 to 1999, the world found eighteen T. rex specimens. From 1999 until now [2008], we've found nine more." Myhrvold has the kind of laugh that scatters pigeons. "We have dominant T. rex market share."

"What I learned from this is that you have to bring in outsiders to help you see beyond your own blind spots," says Reichman. "When we set up the ITDL, we applied this thinking to our model. We didn't care whether ideas, research and products related to 'Innovation in aging' came from inside or outside of Baycrest. We wanted to make the ITDL a petri dish for the best in 'Innovation in aging,' and we wanted to assemble the best teams to develop, refine and validate these advancements no matter where these people came from." This is why a medical institution has strategic partnerships with such diverse organizations as OCAD University (formerly the Ontario College of Art and Design) and the Royal Ontario Museum, among many others.

A common problem with the elderly is that they are constantly being shuttled between their residences and hospitals as they get treated for illnesses or have simple things like their blood pressure taken. "It is very expensive for a health care system to manage the wellness of the elderly this way," says Reichman. "In the future, we are going to look back at this logistical nightmare and wonder how a health care system could sustain such a time-consuming and expensive way to treat seniors. It is far more cost-effective to take health care to where seniors live than to bring seniors to health care. One of the challenges that the ITDL is working on right now is how to embed technology in seniors' homes and modify the processes for treating them so that they don't actually have to leave their homes. Improving this process can cut hundreds of billions of dollars of health care costs around the world, not only in the treatment of the elderly, but in the treatment of all people who require medical care."

VHA: "How Do We Inspire Our Employees to Be More Creative?"

While most companies want to be innovative, it isn't always easy to do. Just declaring to your staff that you want them to be more innovative and creative isn't enough. You need to create a formal infrastructure for innovation so that there is a disciplined process for making it happen and to propagate it throughout the organization.

VHA created a program called Ideas to Action/Innovation as its means of generating creativity—of the sort that leads to meaningful change—within the organization. This program is open to any employee in the organization. It challenges them to research something new or to create a new program for its clients. "More independence" is the decision-making guide for this innovation program. Any employee who wants to participate in the Ideas to Action/Innovation program has to justify their idea when describing in detail how it will create "More independence" either inside or outside of VHA.

Falls are a leading cause of injury for elderly people. With a rapidly aging population, the incidence of injury from falls is only going to increase. The hospitalization and treatment costs for a senior who breaks a bone, or worse, in a fall are extremely high. This is but one of the factors that is causing great strain on the health care system. And if people have extended hospital stays and recuperation periods as a result of falls, it obviously significantly reduces their independence.

At VHA, staff members asked, "What if we could change the behaviour and capability of seniors in a way that would reduce the number of falls?" This question triggered a new initiative in VHA's Ideas to Action/Innovation program. A multidisciplinary pilot project was initiated in community housing to test this hypothesis. One-hour sessions were run by physiotherapists, occupational therapists and registered nurses, with half the time spent on group exercises and the other half spent on education.

The clients who participated in the program reported higher levels of confidence in their balance, making safety-related improvements in their home environment and managing their risk of falls by going to a doctor to review their medications. In other words, they felt more in balance and were taking more responsibility to reduce the risk of falls around their homes. These are small factors that help reduce the likelihood of falling, which is great for people who are prone to falls because, if they can stay healthy, they will maintain their independence. And the cost of a fall-prevention program is far cheaper than treating people who are injured by falls. The results of this pilot were so encouraging that further trials with larger sample sizes are being planned.

10

New Revenue Streams

Discovering Money Hiding in Your Blind Spot

Every company, including ours, operates with blinders on. For some companies, the blinders are wide; for others, they are narrow. Either way, all you can see is what's inside the blinders.

When you apply the blinder metaphor to a company's sales process, you can really see the value of your Core Proposition in identifying opportunities for business you never imagined. How you define yourself as a company affects how you view the marketplace for sales opportunities. To go to an extreme to make a point, if you sell turbines for GE, you aren't likely to view somebody standing on the sidewalk waving for a taxi as a business opportunity. For the turbine salesperson, somebody waiting for a taxi exists outside their field of vision, while an airplane manufacturer sits squarely within it.

What this means for every company is that there are opportunities for business that are sitting outside of the line of sight. They may have been sitting there for years, or even decades, but because of the way you define your company, you don't see them. Shift the definition of the company—in other words, remove the blinders—and all of a sudden opportunities come into view that you'd never have noticed before.

Paradoxically, providing your company with greater focus through your Core Proposition widens your sales team's field of vision. Eckler, the actuarial firm whose Core Proposition is "A greater degree of certainty," is one of the best examples of a company that discovered new revenue streams this way. When you define yourself as an actuary or as a specialist in defined-benefit pensions, your world is small and getting smaller by the day. But when you define yourself as offering "A greater degree of certainty," all you have to do to generate sales is find companies dealing with uncertainty and contact their CEOs.

Let's start with Baycrest, and its ambitious expansion plans, as our first example of an organization that discovered new revenue streams.

Baycrest: "How Do We Replicate Our Model Around the Globe?"

Baycrest's desire to increase its global influence in the realm of innovation and aging doesn't come without a cost. While the end result of this initiative is better care at a lower cost, it costs a lot of money to create these innovations. "We had to figure out a way to not only innovate, but to generate revenue from our innovations so that we could create even more innovations," says Baycrest CEO Dr. Bill Reichman. "I knew that the Baycrest model of care was a valuable asset, so we created an organization called Baycrest Global Solutions (BGS) to monetize how we take care of seniors. There is a frightening demand around the world for more effective ways to care for seniors, and we knew our model could help solve that problem."

The first step for BGS was to codify the Baycrest model of care. But the international demand for a solution to this problem couldn't wait for the project to be complete, and besides, because Baycrest is constantly innovating its model, this will always be a work in progress. So rather than waiting, Baycrest took its knowledge to where the demand is greatest. "We focused on the Pacific Rim, and China in particular," says Reichman. "China has a massive aging population with very little capability to manage it."

The challenge posed by China's aging population has sparked explosive growth in senior care facilities in that country, but there is very little homegrown expertise on how to provide care for seniors effectively. In the past, children looked after their aging parents, but that's not possible anymore. The adult children of the seniors are moving into the cities to find work, so they don't have the time to look after their parents. Because of their migration, they don't even live in the same location as their parents.

"There is a huge opportunity to replicate Baycrest all across China, not just with government-run facilities, but also with those that are being built by insurance companies that have an obligation to senior care," says Reichman. "Building and financing Baycrests in China wasn't realistic, so we decided to create what is essentially a [system of] licensing for the management of long-term care facilities. The challenge we had to overcome is that we were unknown in China, a problem we solved by creating a relationship with Harvard Medical School in China. This gave us instant credibility there and opened up a lot of doors for us."

One of Baycrest's first clients in China was Peking Union Medical College (PUMC), one of the most prestigious medical schools in the country. "We are training them in geriatric treatment," says Reichman. "We design programs for them, show them how to implement them and then monitor their progress. PUMC has very high credibility and an important relationship with Tsinghua University, one of the top two universities in China, so this gives us a huge opportunity to make an impact on geriatric care in the largest country in the world."

Baycrest created another important strategic partnership with Perkins Eastman, a huge developer that had been operating in China for three generations. Perkins Eastman has taken a particular interest in the building of senior care facilities, but they are just developers, not operators. "We approach potential clients together with a total solution," says Reichman. "Perkins Eastman builds the facilities and we provide the know-how to run them. Between our strategic partnerships with Harvard and Perkins Eastman—and the help we get from the Canadian government—we had incredible visibility and credibility in China, and people are coming out of the woodwork there to get our expertise.

"We are very excited about the global possibilities for Baycrest Global Solutions," says Reichman. "BGS is in the process of transforming the word *Baycrest* from a noun to a verb! We are at the very beginning of a process of Baycresting long-term care facilities across China."

Eckler: "Should We Capitalize on These Emerging Markets?"

The major trend in the business world that was troubling to Eckler was the evolution from defined-benefit pension plans to defined-contribution pensions. The problem for Eckler was that, while actuaries were critical to the management of defined-benefit pensions, they historically weren't considered to be needed or had a very limited role in the world of defined-contribution pensions. But since defined-contribution benefits was a fast-growing segment of the marketplace, the question was whether there was an opportunity for Eckler to create a new service that would capitalize on this industry shift.

In a classic case of Murphy's Law, companies started to realize that defined-contribution pensions were causing a big problem with their aging employees. These employees didn't have enough money in their pension funds, so they were staying employed long after they should have retired. This inhibited the upward mobility of younger employees who would have been moving up the ladder as older workers retired from the company. The risk to companies was that if younger employees saw their opportunities for advancement blocked, they would leave to take better positions elsewhere.

As a result of this emerging problem, companies realized that they had to take a more proactive role in their employees' retirement plans. "We saw this as a great opportunity to help these companies get their employees into a better position for their retirement," says Jill Wagman. Eckler decided to partner with Hymans Robertson, an affiliate firm in the U.K. that had created a service called Guided Outcomes (GO). GO's purpose is to help employers and employees understand what their financial status will be when they retire and how to change their behaviour now so that they have enough money for the future.

"The potential for this service is huge," says Wagman. "There are so many companies with thousands or tens of thousands of employees who have underfunded defined-contribution accounts. Each person's account needs to be analyzed individually to determine if they are prepared for their retirement. For those who aren't, and that's likely most of them, we need to guide them on how to change their behaviour now—how to save more money—so that they are not forced to work longer than they want to."

Since defined-contribution pension plans are the plan of future for most private-sector employers, and the problem that needed solving was well defined (and certain), Eckler's decision to launch GO in Canada was made with a great degree of certainty.

Bloom Burton & Co.: "How Can We Get the Big Boys to Partner with Us?"

A challenge for Bloom Burton is that it is a boutique firm that often finds itself competing against some of the biggest investment banks in North America. "Even when we are better, [prospects] would often leap over us to the big U.S. firms because they had the size and the powerful brands," says Jolyon Burton. "They would have seen us as too small. Or they would already be engaged with one of the big firms doing banking and financing, so why did they need us?"

How do you compete against the size and reach of these companies when you are a David in the presence of many Goliaths? "Now when they hear our 'Faster path to monetization' story, they see the broader value of what we do and it gives us the opportunity to be a junior partner to the big firms when these companies moved to the U.S.," says Burton. "They recognize that there are aspects of our services that help to position themselves better with the big firms, so they engage us to provide either preparatory services or services that they can't get from the big firms."

As a boutique firm, being a junior partner to the big U.S. firms creates two fantastic opportunities for Bloom Burton: it has access to business—and revenue—that wasn't available to it before and, from a reputational standpoint, to be seen as working in partnership with the big firms significantly increases the company's credibility as a player in this field. No amount of money could enhance the value of Bloom Burton's brand as much as being in bed with some of the biggest investment banks in the world.

Baycrest: "How Do We Productize and Commercialize Our Know-how?"

Hospitals are not typically in the business of developing and commercializing products, but this is another area in which Baycrest is expanding to fulfill its mandate of "Innovation in aging."

"We created Cogniciti as the commercialization company for products developed at Baycrest," says Dr. Bill Reichman. "We know there is going to be huge demand in the future from both institutions and consumers for products that help maintain brain health. We have the resources and expertise at Baycrest to be at the forefront of this emerging market. We co-founded Cogniciti with MaRS Discovery District, an innovation catalyst founded by the Ontario government, so we could each benefit from the other's expertise in developing these products and bringing them to market. We know how to create the products, and MaRS knows how to scale the business to reach the market."

Cogniciti's first product is a web-based cognitive assessment program that teaches you about your brain and how to keep it healthy. You take a test, which was developed in partnership with Cambridge Brain Sciences Inc. at Western University in London, Ontario, which measures your level of cognitive functioning. The test produces two reports: one for you and one for your doctor. These reports give you guidance on how to deal with the results with your doctor.

"This product is still in the beta stage," says Reichman. "With Cogniciti, we are learning as we go along because developing products is a nontraditional function for an institution like ours. However, the market for brain health products is expected to continue to grow, and there is no reason why an organization with Baycrest's skill set and resources can't be a leader in this for-profit field. With MaRS and Cambridge Brain Sciences Inc., we have excellent development partners. And with Zoomer and the Canadian Association of Retired People, we have two excellent market-testing partners."

11

Sales

Bringing Home More Bacon

At the beginning of this book, we explained how the question "Why should I choose you?" has implications for much more than just marketing, communications and sales. In this chapter, we will focus on how the answer to this question makes sales come faster and easier.

In order to understand how your Core Proposition and Core Story can make sales come faster and easier, it is important to consider how we listen when we are receiving a sales pitch. One of the reasons people obsess so much over the development of a sales pitch is because they want to control the message. They are trying to find the most resonant and relevant points about their product and present them in the most compelling way so that they feel like they have given the sales effort their best shot.

What they don't realize is that the structure of their sales pitch cedes control of the message to the listeners, the people contemplating buying the product or service. The traditional sales pitch is a PowerPoint presentation laden with information about the product's features and benefits. "Here's feature number one and its associated benefits . . . Here's feature number two and its associated benefits . . ." And so on. And because they want to make the strongest possible argument in favour of a sale, they load the pitch document with as many features and benefits as possible. The belief is that not all features and benefits will resonate with every client, but as long as you have enough of them in there, the listeners will find *something* they like.

This is exactly the problem with barfing out a whole bunch of facts and figures about a product in a sales pitch: you leave it to the listener to figure out what's in it for them. The listener has to process everything you present and then decide how what you are offering is relevant to them. These sales pitches don't answer the question "What's the big picture here for me if I buy this product or service?" You've given the prospect all of the details, but you haven't tied it up into a nice, neat and tidy, big-picture bow for them. So they have to figure that out for themselves.

As an example, let's look at Interiors, the retail shelving company whose Core Proposition is "Opening sooner." Prior to its Blueprint, it would pitch new business on the basis of the quality of its project management, employee training/performance, customer service, etc. In other words, its version of features and benefits. Even if all of its competitors didn't pitch on the same basis (and they do!), it is left to the buyer to answer the question "What's in it for me if I choose this company?" You don't want the buyer asking that question, because it means they have ultimate control over the sales pitch. If you leave it to them to answer the most important question—"What's in it for me?"—you have lost control of the most important part of the sales pitch.

This is exactly the conundrum Interiors found itself in with its pitches prior to its Blueprint. We now know that the answer to "What's in it for me?" for a buyer of Interiors' services is "Opening sooner." This is the big-picture answer. All of the features and benefits of what Interiors does serve to support, or prove, that Core Proposition. We are not saying that features and benefits aren't important; it's just that they lose their power when the "What's in it for me?" answer isn't there to lend them context. "Opening sooner" creates the big-picture context for the buyer to understand the significance of the details (the features and benefits).

To sum up what we have just said, there are two ways to manage how a buyer listens to your sales pitch. And they happen to be polar opposites.

> **The traditional way:** I'm going to tell you everything I can about my product (features and benefits) and then leave it to you to decide what is relevant to you.
> **The Blueprint way:** I'm going to tell you what's relevant to you, and then I'm going to tell you things about my product (features and benefits) that prove its relevance.

We have to admit that when we read the part in the second point that says, "I'm going to tell you what's relevant to you," it sounds arrogant because we are deciding what's relevant to somebody else. And it assumes that all of the somebody elses—all potential buyers—find relevance in the same thing about what you do. The reality is that if you define who you are accurately, there is ultimately only one thing in what you do that is relevant to all buyers, as well as to all other stakeholders.

To understand why the statement in the Blueprint way isn't arrogant, let's look at how Interiors structured its sales pitches after its Blueprint. It would start with a preamble that recognized the importance of meeting the store's deadline for opening and the challenges the buyer (the VP of Construction) faced if those deadlines weren't met. This is where "Opening sooner" is introduced. During this preamble, the VP of Construction's head is usually nodding in appreciation that Interiors understands the real stresses and strains he or she faces on a day-to-day basis. At the end of the preamble, the idea of "Opening sooner" is firmly planted in the buyer's brain as the big-picture answer to the question "What's in it for me?"

Now that we have embedded the "What's in it for me?" answer in the buyer's brain at the beginning of the sales pitch, they use that as a filter through which they listen to everything else you are going to say. So the spoken and unspoken dialogue in an Interiors pitch would go something like this:

INTERIORS. [*Preamble that sets the tone with "Opening sooner."*]

VP OF CONSTRUCTION'S INNER VOICE. "If I get the store open sooner, we can start selling sooner and everyone will think I'm a hero."

INTERIORS. "Let me tell you about our project management process . . ."

VP OF CONSTRUCTION'S INNER VOICE. "I can see how the project management process he is describing helps get me to open sooner."

INTERIORS. "Now, here's how we do employee training to ensure the quality of their work . . ."

VP OF CONSTRUCTION'S INNER VOICE. "Yup, I can see how that kind of training leads to employees who work faster and better."

Once Interiors has embedded "Opening sooner" in the buyer's mind, the buyer relates all of the subsequent information (features and benefits) back to the notion of opening sooner. Because the message of "Opening sooner" is so powerful in the buyer's mind, it enhances the value of all of the features and benefits that support it.

We have said elsewhere in the book that features and benefits are no longer enough. That doesn't mean they are of no value as sales tools. It's just that presenting them on their own isn't enough anymore because the world is awash in features and benefits. And for the most part, they come across as generic or as empty claims when they try to stand on their own.

Let's take a look at how Bloom Burton transformed the way in which many of its stakeholders listened to its sales pitch.

Bloom Burton & Co.: "How Do We Broaden the Value People See in Us?"

Prior to its Blueprint, "Why should I choose you?" was the single most frustrating question the people at Bloom Burton had to answer on a daily basis. "We had a bunch of services that people saw as silos," says Brian Bloom. "We had a fragmented story that confused people. What was most frustrating was knowing that we did a great job of helping our clients, but we couldn't communicate that in our story.

"When we restructured and repackaged our story around 'A faster path to monetization,' we shifted from selling services to promising an outcome, listening to our prospect's needs and then packaging the appropriate services for them. We got a completely different reaction to our new story. For the first time, people recognized we have a much broader service offering that delivered much more value."

Bloom and his co-founder, Jolyon Burton, attend J.P. Morgan's annual health care conference in San Francisco. "It is like speed-dating for investors and companies looking for investment," says Burton. "You sit down with these companies looking for investment and you can just see the weariness in their eyes from hearing the same pitch over and over again from companies like ours. I can't tell you how gratifying it was to tell them our story and have them respond with comments like 'Well, this makes so much sense!' or 'I had no idea you had such a robust platform' or 'I had no idea you provided all of the services.' Because they understood the breadth of what we did and its value so fast, we were quickly able to move past the explanation of who we are and begin to engage in a conversation about what their needs are and how we can help them. This made our sales process way more efficient.

"Our new story really accelerated the sales process for us. We saw it work for us at the J.P. Morgan event in San Francisco. We met two hot companies that really interested us. In the past, we would've pitched one of our services, which would've made us seem like a one-dimensional company. Now when we pitch 'A faster path to monetization,' they see how all the services fit together to their benefit."

Momentum: "How Do I Captivate Investors When I Can't Even Talk to Them Face to Face?"

Momentum CEO Drew McDougall got an important introduction to a large foreign investment fund. He had never met the people running the fund, so he didn't have any personal or business history with them to give him credibility. All he had to make a good first impression was the power of his story.

"We sent the white paper to the investor prior to our first phone call with him," says McDougall. "In the first call, I told him the story of the white paper in my own words. He immediately got the concept and was intrigued enough by it that the conversation quickly turned to how they could get involved, [without my] having to explain it more. I can't tell you how valuable it is to get past the story quickly and into the meat of the conversation of how we can do business together. A sales story based on the Core Proposition accelerates the pace of the sales process, shortening it because you hook people immediately and they are now talking to you from a position of intrigue, not skepticism."

On the basis of a white paper and a few phone calls, this deal got right to the due-diligence phase. The power, logic and brevity of the story gave McDougall instant credibility in the eyes of this investor and created a great start to the trust-building phase of this business relationship. Of course, having a great idea and a great story for a start-up isn't enough to close a deal of this magnitude. But the level of interest that McDougall generated right out of the gate, and the speed with which the conversation got to the negotiating stage, is a dream come true for a new company.

The power of the story doesn't stop there. There are two tracks to this negotiation: the funding of McDougall's current project and the possibility of licensing this idea to foreign countries. Keep in mind that McDougall has yet to meet this investor face to face.

Longo's: "How Do We Get People to Buy into the Longo's Way?"

When the word *sales* is mentioned, most people think of selling products or services. What is less obvious is that all of us are constantly selling. We want people to return our emails and phone calls, we want them to attend our meetings, we want them to accept our proposals and we want them to integrate our feedback into what they are doing. This is all selling, too. Sales is more than getting people to buy our products and services; it is getting them to do what we want, when we want them to do it.

"Our senior leadership team created our Core Proposition, and we were the ones who decided this had to be the company's mantra going forward," says Anthony Longo. "But that doesn't mean our employees will automatically buy in." Longo and his senior team had to go out and sell it into the company so that people would buy into it and embrace it not just as the company's mantra, but as their own. "We had a meeting with 450 store managers. When we presented 'Treating you like family' as the Longo's North Star, we knew immediately that it resonated because we could just see the light bulbs going off above their heads. We were able to spend less time explaining it to them, and more time discussing the fullness of what it means and hearing their suggestions on what we should do as a company to expand this idea."

Longo's also uses "Treating you like family" in its recruiting and its orientation program for new hires. "When we are recruiting new people, we proudly state that the cause we are committed to is 'Treating you like family,'" says Longo. "Prospects are very clear about what they are stepping into and if their values are aligned with ours. And when we use 'Treating you like family' to guide our hiring, it is far easier for us to determine in an interview if a prospect's values are aligned with ours. Once people are hired, we take them through an orientation session that is designed around 'treating you like family.' This gets them up to speed faster because we are using simple language with a clear meaning to communicate a thought process that is aligned with our values as embodied in our Core Proposition."

Momentum: "How Do I Make My Website a More Compelling Sales Tool?"

As a start-up developer, virtually everyone Drew McDougall met on behalf of his company was new to his idea. That meant he was making a first impression with everyone who might be instrumental to the realization of his dream. So the importance of having a clear, concise and compelling story can't be underestimated. If he couldn't tell people a story that they could understand quickly and be inspired by, he risked having people walk away who might otherwise fall in love with his idea.

A website was critical to disseminating his message about his new company's unique idea. "When we first started creating our website, we were embarrassed," says McDougall. "It didn't reflect the value of what we were creating, nor the sophistication of our potential customers." Downsizers are reasonably affluent because they are selling the family home and buying a smaller, less expensive place to live. The equity they have tied up in their homes will be used to buy a condo, setting aside what's left over to fund the next phase of their lives.

While the website can be built to serve many functions, most companies use it as essentially an electronic brochure to communicate information about their businesses. Two important reasons people visit a company's website are to get information and to assess the credibility of the business. The combination of the quality of the content on the website and its design are critical elements in establishing credibility in the visitor's mind. People will make important judgments about a company, rightly or wrongly, just on the basis of a quick scan through a website. For this reason, it is critical that the website make a strong first impression so that it succeeds in bringing people in rather than pushing them away.

"Our Core Proposition gave a strong focus for the development of our website," says McDougall. "We knew what to write, and our designer got a good sense of how to present our brand from the Core Story. I got validation as to the power of our website from a fellow developer who asked me who wrote our website because it was so good. I did, and much of it was a cut and paste from our Core Story. We were so proud when we launched our new website—we were not embarrassed by it anymore. And it gave us such a lift to see how well represented we were online."

Bloom Burton & Co.: "How Do We Generate More Sales from Existing Clients?"

Raising money for investment funds is never easy, even when you have a credible track record and the purpose of the fund is seen as valuable. "In the past, we would've gone out and pitched investors on the fund and what it would be used for," says Brian Bloom. "This is the traditional way to raise money. We would have mentioned the other parts of the business in the sales process, but because [these features] seemed disjointed and unrelated, the investors couldn't see how they were connected. In our old story, investors didn't see how our other services added value to the funds. What is interesting is that even *we* didn't see clearly how our other services added value to the funds.

"Now we pitch the funds within the context of 'A faster path to monetization,' and investors see how our services are integrated with, and supportive of, the funds. This gives the funds greater value and makes them easier to sell. Not only do investors see the value, *we* see the value. The confidence we got from seeing how all of our services added value to the fund meant that if somebody didn't invest, it was likely because they didn't want to put their money in health care or biotech, not because they didn't want our fund. In other words, we weren't losing a sale because we didn't have a compelling story; we just weren't the right fit for that investor."

12

After the Blueprint

Training Wheels and Beyond

The best way to predict the future is to create it.

PETER DRUCKER

The colloquial way we describe a Blueprint is that it creates a new future for an organization to live in. You have to describe your destination first, and then do everything in your power to get there. All of the chapters in this book so far have described how to paint a picture of that new future and provide specific direction for how to get there. In this chapter, we will talk about the key success factors in making a Blueprint come to life.

When we talk to CEOs who are considering Blueprinting their organizations, we tell them bluntly that this is not a process for somebody who is considering incremental change. Doing a better job at your current level requires incremental change. Getting to the proverbial next level requires transformation. Blueprinting is a process for transformation.

The Chinese have a proverb that says, "Be careful what you wish for." The warning behind this proverb is that although you may really want something, you must be mindful of its implications, which may not always be what you expected. The same is true of a Blueprint. You may want to transform your organization to get to the next level, but you must be aware of the extraordinary effort it takes to get there.

"It must become a way of life," says Anne Martin, CEO of United Van Lines. "You can't just sit in church. You have to live the life," says Carol Arnett, CEO of VHA Home HealthCare. It takes continuous hard work, not just a big bang at the beginning. What you are transforming the organization into requires ongoing nurturing. It is like gas in a car. The car will only stay in motion for as long as you continue to put fuel in the tank.

The process of implementing a Blueprint is unique for every organization. However, there are three common themes that were mentioned by every CEO we interviewed for this chapter. They are:

Conviction. As a leader, or a leadership team, you must have total conviction in your Blueprint.

Commitment. You must have a full commitment to everything that needs to be done for a successful implementation.

Buy-in plan. You need to get buy-in at every level of the organization.

Conviction

Passion for a goal doesn't guarantee success,
but without it, you can't even begin.

ROSABETH KANTER, CHAIR OF THE HARVARD UNIVERSITY ADVANCED

LEADERSHIP INITIATIVE

Brian Bloom, the CEO of Bloom Burton, expressed the need for total conviction the most vigorously. "You must have 100 per cent conviction or people around you will be able to read that you aren't totally committed," says Bloom. "If you are only at 80 per cent, you have to figure out a way, as the leader, to get yourself to 100 per cent or revise your Blueprint until you get to 100 per cent conviction. People aren't stupid; they will see right through you if you don't have 100 per cent conviction."

Jaime Watt, the CEO of Navigator, believed in his Blueprint but was uncomfortable with the articulation of his Core Proposition, "When you can't afford to lose." He felt the sentiment was accurate, but he wasn't comfortable with the wording. So although he had conviction in his Blueprint, his hesitation about the language meant he wasn't behind it 100 per cent. The result was that his Blueprint lay dormant for about a year. During that period, we had regular monthly breakfasts with Watt, spending a portion of each talking about his discomfort with "When you can't afford to lose."

One of our suggestions was that he talk to people who know him and know the company about the Core Proposition and the underlying story. When he talked to outsiders about "When you can't afford to lose," the reaction was virtually unanimous: it fit both him and Navigator to a tee. The more he heard that, the more comfortable he got with the expression. After about a year of uncertainty, he completely switched his opinion of Navigator's Core Proposition. Like everyone else, he believed that it truly captured what Navigator and its people were all about.

In other words, although it had taken a year, he got to 100 per cent conviction. What followed was a full rollout of his Blueprint. What was unusual in Navigator's Blueprint was that there was very little operational change the company had to make. It was firing on all cylinders except for the story that it told internally and externally. All it needed to do to get to the next level was change its story to reflect what it truly does. Navigator completely overhauled its marketing and sales efforts, which has resulted in a steady and substantial increase in business.

Brian Bloom and his co-founding partner at Bloom Burton, Jolyon Burton, were totally sold on their Blueprint right from the beginning. "Nobody in our company doubted our conviction about the Blueprint," says Burton. "Everybody understood we were dead serious about it and that we believed in it with every fibre of our being. They took it seriously because we took it seriously. This made it much easier for us to achieve buy-in throughout the organization and make the necessary changes that were identified in our Blueprint."

Commitment
Good business leaders create a vision, articulate the vision, passionately own the vision, and relentlessly drive it to completion.

JACK WELCH

You may think that conviction and commitment are essentially the same, but they aren't, and the difference is critical to the successful implementation of a Blueprint. Conviction is how you feel towards something. Commitment is the level of effort you put into making it happen. You need conviction first and then commitment, because it is too easy to abandon commitment when there isn't enough conviction.

Once you have 100 per cent conviction in your Blueprint, you need 100 per cent commitment at all levels of the organization to make it successful. Having said that, commitment starts at the top. When the top demonstrates commitment, it dramatically increases the likelihood that every other level of the organization will become committed.

"The implementation of your Blueprint is an ongoing commitment," says Jacqui Tam, former Assistant Vice-President, Communications, Public Affairs and Marketing, at Wilfrid Laurier University (WLU). "It can't be thought of as a traditional campaign with a start and finish aimed at a specific 'sales' objective. It has to be constantly promoted and reinforced, not because this is something that is unique to a Blueprint, but because it is necessary for anything you want ingrained in your culture."

But what does commitment mean?

Mostly, commitment means having a fully thought-through plan for the implementation of the Blueprint and the will to carry it through. This plan will have two elements to it:

> **Organizational changes:** the shifts that need to be made in how the company operates in order to make sure that everything it does is aligned with the Blueprint
>
> **Communications changes:** the shifts that need to be made in how the company communicates externally (branding, marketing, sales, online) and internally (communications with employees, board members, investors, suppliers, strategic partners and any other relevant stakeholders)

As with any plan, the implementation plan for a Blueprint requires initiatives, timelines, milestones, assigned responsibilities and measurable results. These will look different for each company, but the reason we listed all of these elements is to demonstrate that it requires a full-blown plan. And as with all full-blown plans, it requires somebody to lead the project and, in larger organizations, other people who are involved in making the plan. If you don't treat it with this level of seriousness, people will see that you aren't committed and will treat it as a flavour-of-the-month project. If this happens, the Blueprint is dead.

One of the first steps in executing the Blueprint at a large manufacturing company was to present it to its executive team. People were brought in from across the country for this presentation, and the meeting lasted about two hours. The CEO concluded this meeting by telling his most senior executives he wanted them to implement the Blueprint in every area of their business. That was the full extent of the execution plan. It sent a message to the senior leadership team that there was no serious commitment to this Blueprint, and it died in that moment.

"You need to get your house in order first before going external," says Tam. "You need a comprehensive plan for your operations and communications before you begin to sell it internally and externally. If you treat it only as a communications exercise, it won't work. The implementation of our Blueprint was not a campaign, per se; it is the ongoing recognition of and nurturing of a way of being."

Gaining Buy-in

A genuine leader is not a searcher for consensus but a moulder of consensus.   DR. MARTIN LUTHER KING, JR.

At first blush, the distinction that Dr. King makes seems more semantic than substantive. But the difference between searching for consensus—or buy-in—and moulding it is critical. The searcher is on a journey, in the course of which he or she hopes to find an outcome. The moulder is achieving the outcome by design. In other words, a comprehensive plan has been created for the specific purpose of gaining buy-in. While all of the major themes in this chapter are interconnected—meaning success can't be achieved if any one of them is absent—gaining buy-in is the single most important step in the implementation of the Blueprint.

There are two levels of buy-in that are important to the success of the Blueprint, and they happen in the following order:

1. "I understand what this is about and I agree to work towards making it successful."
2. "I have fully embraced this new idea and it is now an organic part of my way of being in this organization."

It is important to understand that this is a linear progression so that you as a leader or as part of a leadership team don't have unrealistic expectations. At the first level, you want people to buy into the Blueprint and hopefully even be inspired by it. Buying in will begin the process of people changing their thinking and behaviour, both individually and as a group. They will begin to take the actions and use the language outlined in the Blueprint. As they experience the success of these actions and the language, it will give them positive reinforcement that the Blueprint works. This, in turn, will inspire them to take on more of the actions and language of the Blueprint, which will further reinforce that it works. It is a virtuous circle of trial, reward and repeat that slowly ingrains the Blueprint into the ethos and culture of the organization.

It is similar to wearing a new outfit whose style is a little beyond your comfort zone. When you look in the mirror, you have mixed feelings. On the one hand, you really like it and how it makes you look. On the other hand, you are worried that it is a look that others will think it is too "out there" for you to pull off. But a funny thing happens when you wear it in public. You get a compliment or two that you can tell are genuine. This makes you feel a little bit more comfortable about the outfit, so you venture out wearing it more often. The more you do, the more compliments you get until you slowly come to realize that this outfit *is* you. After a while, you don't think twice about wearing it because it has become a normal and natural part of your wardrobe. And you will also probably buy similar clothing in the future without any hesitation.

Stage one in gaining buy-in is getting everybody to try on the new outfit and see how it feels. You want them to gain experience interacting with the new outfit. If you have conviction in your Blueprint and a full commitment to making it a success, your employees will enter that virtuous circle of trial, reward and repeat. They will see how it makes their jobs easier and, as a result, will use it more . . . to make their jobs even easier.

One of the best examples of this virtuous circle comes from a story we told in a previous chapter about Bloom Burton. Prior to its Blueprint, it would have multiple meetings with prospects just to establish its credibility. Once this credibility phase was complete, it could move on to detailed discussions about how it could help the prospect and about outlining the next steps. After Bloom Burton redesigned its sales pitch to be aligned with the Blueprint, the credibility phase took about ten minutes. In that time, it was able to begin the conversation about a specific course of action that it could take to help the prospect. Bloom Burton was able to go broader and deeper with the prospect much more quickly, making the sales process more efficient and effective— and less expensive.

Stage two is both the successful end state of phase one and the beginning of the never-ending effort to sustain a new ethos. In stage two, people have internalized the Blueprint and are now expressing it as a normal and organic part of their day-to-day thinking and behaviour. As we have said before, it is important that this new way of being be constantly nurtured or else it will wither. As Carol Arnett, CEO of VHA, says, "It's like a shark. It has to keep swimming or it will die. You have to work at it. It won't happen spontaneously or in an ad hoc way. You can't let up."

An interesting thing happened in our first interview with Arnett for this book. At first, she was a little reluctant because she thought VHA hadn't done a great job of implementing its Blueprint. But the more she talked and gave us examples of new initiatives and new ways of thinking within the organization, the more she realized how broadly it had been implemented and how much it had become an organic driver of its culture and operations.

All of the CEOs we interviewed said the same thing about gaining buy-in to the Blueprint:

- Start immediately!
- You need a plan that targets every level of the organization.
- Take a multi-channel approach to the socialization of the Blueprint throughout the organization.

Start Immediately!

You don't learn to walk by following rules. You learn by doing, and by falling over.

RICHARD BRANSON

"My one regret about the implementation of our Blueprint is that we didn't start sooner," says Brian Bloom. "For every minute you delay deploying it, you are losing sales. We only realized this after we implemented our Blueprint and started reaping the rewards. Of course, you have to have a solid plan in place for its execution first. But get started with creating the plan and implementing it as quickly as possible."

Often people are too careful when beginning any kind of initiative. Conventional wisdom dictates that you have all of your ducks in a row before you do something. While we agree with this, you need to strike a balance between planning and speed. "Take the time to prepare," says Jacqui Tam of WLU. "Don't rush, because you have only one chance to make that first impression." The challenge is to create a solid rollout plan without trying to make it perfect. Get to a place where you are confident in the plan, even though you don't necessarily have all the *T*s crossed and the *I*s dotted. As with all plans, it will change as you watch it unfold. You can correct weaknesses in the plan as you go along, and there will always be weaknesses, even in the most comprehensive plans.

Target Every Level of the Organization

Leadership is the art of getting someone else to do something you want done because he wants to do it.

DWIGHT D. EISENHOWER

"You need to socialize the Blueprint from the top down," says Anthony Longo, CEO of Longo's supermarkets. "I think we did a good job of getting buy-in from senior management and store managers. If I were to do it over again, we would have had a more comprehensive program targeting our in-store team members. We left it to the store managers to do that, but what we realized later was that because they were new to the Blueprint, they were learning how to live it at the same time we were asking them to socialize it at the store level. It worked, but just not as quickly and fully as it could have if we had a management team dedicated to getting buy-in from the front lines.

"It is critical that you get the top of the organization on board first," adds Longo. "Every level down you go in socializing your Blueprint, people look to the levels above them to see if they are serious. If they see that their managers are committed to the plan, they will be committed to the plan. So although the Longo's plan was not perfect, it was still successful, in part, because people saw how committed management was to the Blueprint."

Carol Arnett at VHA concurs. "We did a good job of getting buy-in from senior management and at the grassroots level. I think we could've done more at the mid-management level, which would have covered our entire organization." What Arnett implies is that VHA's plan, like Longo's, wasn't perfect, but it was successful anyway. So don't let the quest for perfection interfere with beginning the implementation as quickly as possible.

So far, we have focused on getting buy-in from employees at every level of the company. But for many organizations, there will be many critical stakeholders in addition to employees. These can include:

- Board members (this is especially true for not-for-profits and charities, whose boards often take on a much more hands-on, high-level management role)
- Investors, especially for publicly held companies who must report to their shareholders on a quarterly basis and, more intensively, at their AGM
- The financial community—again, for publicly held companies that need to stay in the good books of analysts and other key players who influence how the company is perceived in the public markets
- Strategic partners, because they play such an important role in growing the business
- Suppliers, a particularly important group for Longo's, the midsize supermarket chain, because they are a strategic asset for a company that is a David among Goliaths

"You need to identify and prioritize your most important stakeholders," says Anne Martin, CEO of United Van Lines. "You need to get them all onside because any one of them can inhibit the implementation of your Blueprint if they aren't aligned." Martin's board was particularly important because of the ownership structure of UVL. The company is a federation of approximately 200 moving companies, each of which is an owner of the "parent" that Martin runs. The board is made up of owners, so it was critical that she get buy-in from them in order to get buy-in from the rest of the owners/members.

For publicly traded companies, a common complaint of the board and shareholders is they don't understand the CEO's vision and they don't have a clear understanding of where the company is going. Since the Blueprint crystallizes the CEO's vision and articulates it in a clear, concise and compelling way, the CEO needs to get buy-in for it from these two groups in order to lead effectively and, more importantly, get them off his or her back.

Suppliers are less obvious stakeholders, but as we pointed out with Longo's, they are often an important strategic asset. Getting their buy-in to the Blueprint gives them a better understanding of what you are trying to achieve with your customers, which enables them to more effectively shape how they provide their products or services to you. Suppliers to food retailers are constantly dreaming up new ideas for food products and pitching them to supermarket executives. Knowing that Longo's Core Proposition is "Treating you like family," suppliers understand that this supermarket chain is looking for food products that have a more traditional, home-cooked style. Armed with this knowledge, food suppliers have two opportunities:

- Specifically design traditional, home-cooked foods and pitch them to what you know is an eager audience for these kinds of meals; or,
- Find ideas that you have already developed that are traditional, home-cooked foods and have been rejected by others, and pitch them to an eager audience at Longo's.

Having its suppliers aligned with its Core Proposition adds value to everything Longo's does for its customers.

The boards of not-for-profits and charities are well-meaning people who have a passion for the mandate of the organization. For example, board members of an organization that is dedicated to an illness such as heart disease or cancer have often been intimately affected by the disease, whether directly or indirectly. They are on the board because they want to spare others from the anxiety, pain and heartache that they experienced. In order for them to have confidence in the CEO and the activities of the organization, they need to be inspired by its mandate. Since these boards often play a bigger role in the management of the organization than does a corporate board, it is important to get them aligned with the Blueprint so that:

- They have confidence in the charity; and
- They play a less intrusive role in the day-to-day management because they have that confidence.

Deans are a critical stakeholder group that is unique to universities. Because of their senior leadership role in their faculties and their tenure, they are extremely powerful. As the leader of the university, if you don't have the deans' support for whatever you want to accomplish, it won't get done. Your initiatives will die before you start. Max Blouw, the president of Wilfrid Laurier University (WLU), had an acute understanding of, and sensitivity to, the importance of the deans' buy-in, so he managed the process with them very carefully and respectfully.

Together we prepared and presented the WLU Blueprint to the deans in a meeting that lasted a full morning. While the presentation itself took only about 20 minutes, the debate lasted over two hours. Their input prompted small but important changes to the Blueprint, all of which were essential to getting their buy-in. In the end, they approved the Blueprint and started integrating it into their day-to-day activities.

The presentation to the WLU deans taught us an important lesson about achieving buy-in. If the Blueprint had been presented to them as a fait accompli, it would have been impossible to get their buy-in. Nobody in a position of power likes to have a plan forced upon them. The Blueprint was presented to them as a draft, so it was understood that it was not complete until they were involved in the development process. We explained to them that only a small core of people could create the draft because the work is so intensive that a larger group would have made the process unwieldy. They understood this point and, in the ensuing conversation, felt heard and respected.

Take a Multi-channel Approach

If you have an important point to make, don't try to be subtle or clever. Use a pile driver. Hit the point once. Then come back and hit it again. Then hit it a third time—a tremendous whack.

WINSTON CHURCHILL

Okay, maybe a tremendous whack is a little extreme! The real point here is it takes a lot for something to sink in and transform how people think and operate (in other words, transform the culture). "You need to create many touch points when you are selling your Blueprint into your organization," says Carol Arnett of VHA. "Changing an element of your culture takes time before it becomes second nature. Among other things, we used town-hall meetings for groups and also had one-on-one sessions for training. In these meetings, we talked about how living the Blueprint would look in their work, we came up with examples of how things would shift and we did some role-play. These tactics were really useful in broadening people's understanding of the Blueprint and how they should apply it in their work."

One of the things that comes out of the Blueprint is language—

words and expressions—that become particular to the organization, not the least of which is the Core Proposition itself. "You need to work the language of the Blueprint into the activities you are doing to gain buy-in. When people start to adopt the language, it changes how they think which, in turn, changes how they act," says Arnett.

Jacqui Tam agrees. "We developed guidelines for how to talk about it so that people knew how to shape the story for different audiences. It is important to create guidelines and not a script, because you don't want people to sound like robots parroting the company line. If you develop good guidelines, people will develop their language in their own words so that it flows naturally from their mouths. In the early stages, people will use the guidelines extensively, but eventually it will become second nature to them. The beauty of guidelines is that they give senior management the confidence that everybody is talking about the organization the same way—and accurately—but they are doing it in their own words so that it sounds credible. In other words, language is strategically managed so that is expressed naturally. We started the sell-in of the Blueprint in September a few years ago, and by the winter session most people in the organization were talking within the context of the Blueprint. It had been internalized and had become an organic element of our culture."

Obviously, the organization's website is one of the most important tools for socializing the Blueprint because it reaches both internal and external stakeholders on a 24/7 basis. Most organizations change the messaging on their website after the Blueprint because they can express their value proposition with much more clarity. When people see the language and the initiatives of the Blueprint on the website, it makes an important statement about the importance of the Blueprint rollout to the organization. Another way of saying this is, if your Blueprint isn't reflected on your website, people will not believe the importance of its role in guiding the organization into its new future. As employees look to see whether management is serious about the Blueprint initiative, having it reflected on the website may be the single most important element in its not being seen as a flavour-of-the-month project.

Anne Martin of United Van Lines is also a fan of the multi-channel approach. "We had a particularly challenging task because we not only had to get buy-in from employees, we had to get it from the owners group as well. We had to get buy-in from approximately 200 owners, all of whom are my bosses, and from all of their employees as well, not just the ones who work for me at head office. One of the first things we did was redesign the website. We had to make the messaging consistent with Core Story for both external and internal audiences. Aligning the website with the Blueprint sent an important message to all of our internal stakeholders that we were serious about putting the Blueprint into play.

"We started the buy-in process at our AGM, where we first introduced the Blueprint to the owners. We conducted workshops at the AGM with the owners to make sure they understood the Blueprint fully and explored ways that it could be manifested throughout the business. This served to make them a part of the planning process, rather than just recipients of the messaging, which is a great way to get buy-in. They were not just hearing about the Blueprint, they were providing advice and suggestions for the best ways to roll it out across the business." This is very similar to what Max Blouw did at WLU when he made the deans a part of the process as a means of gaining their buy-in.

"We then went across the country meeting with the managers of all of the individual moving companies, our members," says Martin. "We conducted round tables so that we could introduce them to the Blueprint, talk to them about how it was going to shift the business and get their input into ways that it could change the company and the culture. We also provided them with materials that would constantly be in front of all of their employees, such as bookmarks, to constantly remind them of the key thrusts of the Blueprint.

"We then had to reach all of the employees in the member companies. So we developed webinars and took them through the same process that the owners and managers went through. An important element of this approach was respecting the politics of the organization. We cascaded the Blueprint from the top of the company to the bottom, and we created an inclusive process that didn't mandate anything on anybody. As a result, nobody got their backs up or provided any serious resistance."

As with Wilfrid Laurier University, UVL had a plan in place that had two streams: the campaign to achieve buy-in throughout the organization; and the implementation of some of the organizational changes, which provided tangible proof that the Blueprint was coming to life. The most important organizational change was introducing a task force infrastructure (described in detail earlier in the book). The major decisions the company had to make were identified by the owner group. These became the subjects of the task forces. An employee-only section of the UVL website became the management tool for the execution of these task forces. Not only did this democratize decision making in the organization, it became very high-profile proof that the company was serious about the implementation of its Blueprint.

Bloom Burton is a much smaller company than the others that have been mentioned in this chapter, so the internal audience from whom they had to get buy-in was much more manageable. However, its implementation plan was as well thought through and sophisticated as that of any big company. "We had to get people to see that this wasn't marketing or communications," says Brian Bloom. "It is a new ethos. It is a new way of existing, and of describing how and why we exist that way. It can't be seen as just cosmetic elements such as branding, logo and advertising. We had to make sure our people understood the gravity of the project.

"Having said the Blueprint isn't about marketing, we introduced it concurrent with a creative reboot. We wanted to make a big splash and to signal a new beginning, both internally and externally. Completely redoing our branding and our corporate identity created a story that we had to tell to our employees and all of our external stakeholders. It gave us the permission to go out and tell people who we are even though they thought they already knew who we are.

"We hired an agency to redesign our corporate identity and to create a new website. We handed them the Blueprint and said, 'This is who we are.' We told the agency to trust the Blueprint, but they constantly wanted to change stuff, to reinvent stuff. I would just say to them, 'The answer to your question is on page 17,' or, 'The answer to that question is on page 4.' We used the Blueprint to keep them on track." If you want to see Bloom Burton's Blueprint, just look on its website. It is an almost verbatim expression of its Blueprint.

Epilogue

Every man gotta right to decide his own destiny.

BOB MARLEY

Control your own destiny or someone else will.

JACK WELCH

Define or be defined.

THOMAS SZASZ

We were privileged to be invited to a small private meeting with one of the richest men in Canada to help him answer the question "Where do I invest next?" He wanted advice on which companies he should buy. We didn't contribute much to the first half hour of the meeting as it unfolded along a traditional track of SWOT (strengths, weaknesses, opportunities and threats) analysis and industry segmentation. After a while, we jumped in and told our host that he was asking the wrong question. We told him he shouldn't be asking, "Where do I invest next?" He should be asking, "What are the strategic guidelines for where I should invest next?" Thus started an eight-month journey with a very interesting man in which we challenged everything that he said and thought to be true in business, and he did the same with equal vigour right back to us. To this day, we have a soft spot in our hearts for this gentleman.

The difference in these two questions is profound. The first question asks, "What, specifically, should I buy?" The second asks, "On what basis do I make those purchase decisions?" The reason he was asking the wrong question is that the order is critical. You first have to know on what basis you are making decisions; from that starting point, you can then ask what decisions are you going to make.

Jumping straight into what decisions to make without having clear, relevant strategic guidelines for decision making is all too common in business. The price a company pays can be small, or it can cost tens or even hundreds of millions of dollars if it is for something like a product the market doesn't want (hello New Coke!). There is no place this is more damaging, or more common, than in determining the future of an organization. The question "Where are we going?" is being contemplated by thousands of companies around the world every day, and it is being done, for the most part, without clear and relevant strategic guidelines. This is why, in most companies, if you asked everyone on the board and all of the senior executives where the organization is going, everyone would have a different answer, some of which would be "I don't know." Having these strategic guidelines would have saved companies like Blockbuster, Kodak and Borders.

There is an old adage that says, "Fail to plan, plan to fail," which implies that if you don't have a detailed plan, you are likely headed for failure. The problem with most companies is that they put together a detailed plan without having high-level strategic guidelines that keep the making of the plan on track. This is like trying to solve a jigsaw puzzle, with thousands of pieces strewn on the table, but no big picture to guide the putting together of the pieces. You can still complete a jigsaw puzzle successfully without the big picture, but it is far more difficult and time-consuming. When a company creates a plan without the big picture, it is also far more difficult and time-consuming. This path is more expensive and creates more confusion in the organization than when you have the big picture clearly in front of everybody.

With clear and compelling strategic guidelines, it's easier to see what you need to do. The clearer and more compelling those strategic guidelines are, the more self-evident the path to a successful future becomes. Blueprinting was created to discover and articulate the guidelines that steer an organization in the right direction. Unlike a traditional strategic plan, it is not meant to lock you into a specific set of steps that will take you stride by stride into the future. The purpose of the Blueprint is to create boundaries for the company. Anything it does within those boundaries is on strategy, while anything it contemplates outside of those boundaries should be discarded. This gives the company enough focus to push forward with a high degree of discipline and alignment, but also enough latitude that it can shift with a marketplace that is evolving at an ever-accelerating pace.

The detailed action plan that follows a Blueprint is very specific. But the reality of this plan is that it is an estimate of what it is going to take to achieve the new future that is defined in the Blueprint. In Neil Young's song "Sugar Mountain," he sings, "Ain't it funny how it feels when you're findin' out it's real?" He's saying that the reality of a situation when you are actually living it can be far different from what you anticipated. Customers, competitors, markets, investors and board members have a funny way of intruding on the best-laid plans of mice and men. So while it is important to have a detailed action plan and the ability to measure your success against it, it is also important to be able to shift and adapt as you see things not working or as you discover better ways of doing things while the plan is in progress.

Without high-level guidelines, it is often very difficult to determine whether or not your shifts and adaptations are appropriate.

Apple faces this problem every day because, although many of its products are market leaders, it isn't the only innovator in its space. Should it adopt innovations that others discover? Should it ignore them? Or should it figure out a way to leapfrog over its competitors' innovations? As Simon Sinek points out in his book *Start with Why*, Apple's guiding principle is "changing the game." In answer to the above questions, as long as what Apple does results in a game-changing product, it is on the right path. If it adopts others' innovations just to catch up or stay on par, it isn't doing enough. In his relentless pursuit of "making a dent on the universe," Steve Jobs would never accept a parity product because "changing the game" was such an organic part of his personality.

A Blueprint is not the only way, by any means, to create long-term, high-level strategic guidelines for a company. It is just one methodology. If you have one takeaway from this book, we hope it is that you see the critical importance of having high-level strategic guidelines shaping everything that you do and say. An excellent starting point for the development of the strategic guidelines is a discussion around the question "Why should I choose you?" In the course of that conversation, you will come up with many answers, but only one will resonate with all of your stakeholders. When you discover that one bold statement—expressed in seven words or less—that resonates with all of your stakeholders, you will have a simple and compelling strategic filter that everyone in and related to your organization will understand and will be able to articulate—one that will guide everything that you do and say from that point on.

APPENDIX 1

The Clarity Test

Clarity at every level of an organization increases the likelihood that it is performing to its potential. Confusion at any level acts as an anchor that slows growth. Here is a short questionnaire to determine whether your growth is being slowed by confusion anywhere in your organization, starting at the top and working down.

If you are the organization's leader, we suggest you do this test yourself, but more important, also give it to each member of your executive team to do anonymously. This will ensure that they have the freedom to answer candidly and will inform you of any blind spots you may have in your evaluation of clarity within your company. Answer each question on a five-point scale, with 1 being "no clarity" and 5 being "complete clarity."

1. Is the CEO clear in his or her own mind about who the company is, where it is going and how it will get there?

If not, it is likely because the CEO believes there are a number of good directions in which a company can go, especially if he or she is new to the position. On top of that, every board member and every member of the CEO's executive team may have ideas about where the company should go and are actively lobbying the leader to follow their recommendations. How to decide which one is right? Whatever confusion the CEO is feeling in this situation, it is around trying to determine the one direction to take the organization when faced with many attractive and achievable options.

O_1　O_2　O_3　O_4　O_5

2. If the CEO has a clear vision in his or her mind, is it articulated in a clear, concise and compelling way so that it is both understood and embraced by the entire board of directors?

Board governance is becoming more and more stringent with each passing year and each new securities scandal. The potential liability of individual board members increases the pressure on them to ensure there is accountability to shareholders and regulators. But how can the board judge the performance of a CEO without knowing exactly where he or she is taking the company? The more clarity a CEO creates about the company's direction, the easier it is to get buy-in from the board and gain its ongoing support.

O_1　O_2　O_3　O_4　O_5

3. If the CEO has a clear vision in his or her mind, is it articulated in a clear, concise and compelling way so that it is both understood and embraced by the entire executive team?

If not, there is confusion within the organization, from the executive team down to the grassroots and beyond. If the executive team is not clear about the CEO's direction for the company, it will make it very difficult for other leaders in the company to a) align their tasks with the company's direction and b) communicate why and how those tasks are aligned with where the company is going.

O 1   O 2   O 3   O 4   O 5

4. Are middle managers crystal clear about the CEO's vision and the purpose of the specific projects developed under the leadership of the executive team?

If not, middle managers will be confused about how to properly lead the execution of the projects developed by the executive team. Middle managers are constantly having to adjust how they execute based on day-to-day realities. The link between major initiatives and the CEO's vision gives them a context in which to implement most effectively.

O 1   O 2   O 3   O 4   O 5

5. Are rank-and-file employees clear about the CEO's vision, the major initiatives created at the executive level and what they are being asked to do by their managers?

If not, there is a good chance that even the most brilliant of visions and strategies will die on the shop floor. To implement the plans of the company most effectively, employees need to be clear on, and inspired by, the company direction. Clarity gives them a sense of purpose and an understanding of how each of their roles makes a material difference in achieving the organization's direction.

O 1   O 2   O 3   O 4   O 5

6. Are customers clear about the purpose of the organization and why they should choose you?

   If not, all of the clarity you have created internally is being compromised by customers' lack of understanding about what you do and why you do it. Being clear about this makes it far easier for them to answer the question "What's in it for me?" when contemplating your product or service, which makes it faster and easier for you to make the sale.

   If you don't have clarity at all six levels, it is likely that your company is underperforming relative to its real potential. The purpose of this book is to help you achieve clarity, at every level of the organization, about who it is and where it is going.

APPENDIX 2

Playing the
"Why Should I Choose You?" Game

We wanted to test an idea. We were looking at a Lexus ad in the paper that was for a single model, not its whole line of cars. Across the bottom, seven local dealers were listed. We realized this gave us a perfect opportunity, because we could conduct an experiment in which all the conditions were identical except for one variable: the dealership. We picked three that were an equal distance from us, knowing that a dealer's first line of differentiation is how close you are to them.

We called up a Lexus dealership and explained to the salesman who answered the phone that there were three Lexus dealerships within a short distance of us. So, all things being equal, we wanted to know why we should buy a car from his particular dealership. To our shock, he said quite indignantly, "In 26 years in this business, I have never been asked that question!"

Was he kidding?

He wasn't! We were shocked by his response for two reasons: first, that a simple, reasonable question would make him so angry; and second, that he thought he had never been asked that question before. What he didn't realize was that he is being asked that question in every single interaction he has with a customer, whether in conversations at the dealership, talking on the phone or devising marketing and advertising designed to lure and close buyers.

You could laugh off his response as a misguided answer, but the reality is that we heard the same thing over and over again from people in companies large and small who are responsible for selling products and services. "Oh, I've never been asked that before" is how we usually heard the answer, but mostly in a polite tone of voice that suggested this was a novel but irrelevant question.

The next Lexus dealer we called was interesting because he started an argument with himself in trying to answer the question.

US. Why should I buy this Lexus from you?

HIM. We have the best service department. No, wait . . . all Lexus dealers have great service departments.

US. (*Silence*)

HIM. We have the best customer service. Actually, all Lexus dealers have great customer service.

US. (*Silence*)

HIM. We buy all of the daily newspapers, we have the best selection of magazines and we serve the finest coffee.

US. (*Silence*)

HIM. The truth is, if I had a good answer to that question, I would be the top salesperson in the country!

We had to admire his honesty . . . and empathize with his frustration. But before we jump all over one of the most successful car companies in the world (Lexus is owned by Toyota) for its lack of sales acumen, let's look at how some other car companies fared.

We called a General Motors dealership and had this conversation:

US. Why should we buy from GM?

HER. GM matches or exceeds all competitors' warranties.

US. Isn't GM's warranty basically the same as others'?

HER. It's really hard to tell you why, in general terms, to choose GM. We have lots of dealerships.

(*She transferred us to a salesperson.*)

HIM. GM offers zero per cent financing, roadside assistance, and these cars are around for a long time.

US. Is that different from other car companies?

HIM. I could go on and on about GM products.

US. Please do . . .

HIM. GM is having problems now, but it is a big ship in a small lake—it's hard to turn around. The new Hondas—nothing against them—but the design in front swoops down, giving less protection in the event of an accident. For durability and protection, the Hondas . . . I didn't mind those cars. I'm not saying their engine is bad. But for protection, value, interest rate, and OnStar, the imports don't have it.

So what does Honda have to say about why we should buy?

HIM. Well . . . because . . . I mean . . . depends what you are looking for. Honda is reputable for our quality, warranty, competitive interest rates.

US (*to ourselves*). Hmm, where have we have heard that before?

HIM. I'm not a salesman. Let me put you through to a salesman.

US (*to salesperson*). Why should I buy a Honda?

HIM. That's a rather wise question . . . Honda offers safety and performance. Open up the *Consumer Reports*. They say the cars are reliable, safe, economic, value for your money. They are non-biased car critics.

US. But can you tell me why I should buy a Honda?

HIM. It's not what I say. Go to the *Consumer Reports*.

US. But you are a salesman. You should be able to tell me why I should buy a Honda.

HIM. It's to each his own. Safe, reliable, economical, appearance, all the factors combined for you to decide if it's right for you.

US. So what is it that makes Honda the best in all of those categories?

HIM. Honda is the best car for the price in the market. Based on reliability, safety. I mean . . . that's a very good question. I can send you an email with the *Consumer Reports*. Or you have to search the *Consumer Reports*.

US. So the *Consumer Reports* are better to find out why I should choose Honda than calling you at Honda?

HIM. People buy Honda for five reasons: value for their money, safety, reliability, great fuel economy, cost of ownership/depreciation.

So even Honda, one of the most venerable and successful car companies in the world, struggles with articulating a compelling, differentiating reason to buy. Let's look at Chrysler, a company that has come out with some of the most quirky, innovative car designs of the past decade in spite of its financial troubles.

US. Why should I buy a Chrysler?

HIM. It's a North American car manufacturer. Making the best SUV, best 4x4 and a variety of products.

US. What is it that is better about Chrysler's products?

HIM. There are so many products out there.

US. So why would I want to choose Chrysler over another company?

HIM. I'm not going to speak about other products.

US. That's fine. But what is it about Chrysler that makes it better? What do you like about it?

HIM. I'm used to it. I sell it. I'm safe. I haven't bought it yet; I drive a company car. It's an individual choice, everyone's different. I dunno . . . who you are, what you are looking for? Basically, we are one of . . . everyone's making a nice product. Depends on you and what you like to drive.

But how will I know that "what I like to drive" is a Chrysler if Chrysler can't tell me what is likeable about driving its cars? Let's see if a higher-end brand like BMW can articulate a compelling reason to buy its cars.

US. Why should I choose BMW over another brand?
HIM. It's probably one of the most amenable [sic] products. For performance, luxury and driver experience. Scheduled maintenance is covered for four years. It's the best warranty in the industry.
US. So what am I getting for the money I spend?
HIM. Value, luxury brand, solid design, and the fit and finish. There's a 12-year warranty on rust.
US. What would you choose as the number one thing about BMW?
HIM. Road manner. The handling and it's easy to drive. Performance and power, you can feel it in the turns, it sticks to the road. Why you should choose BMW: drive it.

BMW is a mythical brand. There is a romance to BMW that goes far beyond being a transportation device that gets you from point A to point B. The magic of this brand is all about how it makes you feel and how it feeds your sense of self-identity. BMW is a badge that you proudly wear when you drive this brand and it broadcasts to the world a status you have achieved. None of this is captured in the salesman's answer to our most basic of questions: "Why should I choose you?"

So can anyone answer this question for us? Let's look at airlines, starting with United Airlines.

US. Why should I choose United Airlines over another airline?
UNITED (*after an uncomfortable pause*). Uh, my system is down and my computer is being rebooted. It may take a few moments. I'm going to put you on hold.

About three minutes later, she returned.

UNITED. Depends on the price. You have to find the price of other airlines.
US. So aside from your prices, is there any other reason to choose United Airlines?
UNITED. You can make your reservation and hold for 24 hours while you check prices. The service with United is comfortable seats and big planes. There is more choice of seats and the seats are bigger and more space.
US. The benefit of flying with United Airlines is that you have better seats?
UNITED. Other airlines provide less [*i.e., a lower*] price. But then they give you a bench to sit on top of for ten dollars.

None of the answers given above by United, nor any you will see below by any of the other airlines, reflects the totality of the travel experience and where the flight fits into the larger context. For instance, if you are going on vacation, the flight could be the beginning of reconnecting with your family, relief from the stresses of work or experiencing a new adventure in an exotic location (or all of the above). The airline is delivering you to this experience so, considering the larger context, there is much more to the flight than just comfortable seats or lower prices. The airline is a partner in something that is essential and enjoyable in your life, yet its sales narrative reflects none of these important elements. If it did, you may be less concerned about the few dollars you save with airline A versus airline B because you feel like airline B is going to make your vacation experience so much better.

Let's see how American Airlines does.

US. Why should I choose American Airlines over another airline?
AMERICAN. Well, there are a variety of different reasons. It's personal preference. Different markets are served by different airlines.
US. What is it about American Airlines that is better for serving its market than others?
AMERICAN. We have a variety of non-stop flights, an Elite class, first class and business class. Also newer aircraft. Life expectancy is reached (*approximately 20 years?*) and they are sold to other airlines; beyond the standard 14-point aircraft inspection.
US. What do you see as the number one reason to choose this company?
AMERICAN. Quality of service. Not to say you can't find customer service elsewhere. The seating is comparably comfortable and all of our representatives are based in the U.S., not in other countries.
US. Do you have a motto?
AMERICAN. "Our lowest fare guaranteed." People don't have time to shop around, but if you find a lower price after purchase, we will give you a price adjustment and a $50 travel voucher.

Is a European airline better at giving us a compelling reason to fly with them? Let's try British Airways.

US. Why should I choose British Airways over another airline?
BA. Our reputation and service. I've never been asked that before. We are a premium airline. We offer a fully flat bed seat.

US. What would you identify as the number one reason to choose British Airways?

BA. The food, service and staff. I'll read you what the website says . . . [*Reads directly from website*] I don't really know what to tell you.

So apparently, British Airways is no better. The airline experience is typical in that every airline offers the same standard set of features and benefits, and claims that it does it better than anyone else. So it isn't surprising that American and United talk about comfortable seats and quality service; not only are these two qualities as generic as they come in the airline business, but anyone who has flown any of these airlines knows that their seats are actually quite uncomfortable compared to what we sit on at work and at home on a daily basis. "Comfortable" seats in airline parlance is definitely a relative term. And all premium airlines that do long-haul travel have seats that convert to beds as a standard feature in first class. This is by no means a differentiating feature or something that makes an airline uniquely remarkable.

Every one of these companies was missing the larger context. None of the airlines saw, nor did they communicate, how they fit into the bigger picture of the customer experience. When you think about all of the examples we have illustrated above, this is true for every one of the companies we called. Instead of understanding the larger context of the buying experience, and appreciating the far more important role they play with their customers, all of these companies are pushing generic details to sell themselves. They make vague, generic promises of more comfortable seats or friendlier service or a better warranty—or lower prices, which is the most dangerous of all claims—when there is a much stronger platform from which they could be selling: what makes them uniquely remarkable. As a result, they are mired in a war of irrelevant details with their competitors, spending billions and billions of dollars on marketing and communications campaigns that, from the customer's standpoint, miss the point.

Everyone Is in Sales

Make no mistake: *every* employee in the world is involved in their companies' sales processes in one way or another, so being able to answer the question "Why should I choose you?" is a critical responsibility we all share. Yet almost nobody can answer that question in a clear, concise and compelling way.

If you don't believe us, try it out for yourself. The next time you are buying something, ask the salesperson why you should buy from them. This question typically returns one of two answers. The first is a blank stare, the classic deer-in-the-headlights look, because they have no answer. As you look into their eyes, you can almost see and hear the cogs in their brains grinding as they try to grapple with this simple but foreign question. The second type of answer is the motor-mouth response. They talk and talk and talk, thinking that a long string of verbiage will make them sound intelligent, when in fact it just exposes that they don't have an answer. Ironically, they will usually conclude the monologue with the question "Does that answer your question?" because they can see from the look in your face—and because they recognize in their own confused response—that it doesn't.

If you play the "Why should I choose you?" game, our estimate is that 98 per cent of the people will give you one of the two unconvincing responses described above. The other 2 per cent will say something useful. This is not an indictment of the salespeople! They are not stupid. Many of them are, in fact, very intelligent. They just haven't been given the tools by their companies to explain to customers in a clear and compelling way why you should buy from them and not from the competitor down the street.

Let's look at a few more examples of the responses we got to the question "Why should I choose you?" from over 100 companies we talked with in doing research for this book.

Computers

We were buying laptops for the office. The first company we called was Dell, which used to have one of the most unique and compelling value propositions in the technology business: buy over the phone, and what we save in avoiding the huge costs of supporting a retail sales channel, we will pass on to you. We called the toll-free number and explained to the salesperson that we knew very little about buying computers and asked why we should choose Dell over a multitude of competitors.

He said that Dell listens very carefully to our specific needs and then custom-builds computers from scratch, just for us. "We don't just send you a computer that has been sitting on the shelf for months," he explained. "We build one fresh for you." We didn't realize that, like melons, "freshness" was important to the purchase decision, but we thanked him for what seemed at the time like a great answer. We let him know that we would call back if we were going to buy from Dell.

We then called HP and MDG and asked them the same question—and got exactly the same "custom-built computer" response as we got from Dell. So we phoned back the same salesperson at Dell and told him about our experience with the other two companies. We explained to him that we felt stuck in the same place we were in when we started: we didn't know how to choose a supplier because they all seemed to offer the same thing. There didn't seem to be a compelling reason to choose one way or another.

So we threw the ball back into his court and asked him again why we should choose Dell. Here is how that conversation went:

HIM. Ask your friends.

US. But you are the person who has been specifically trained to explain to us why we should buy from Dell.

HIM (*after a long, uncomfortable pause*). The screws we use to bolt our components into our computers are stronger than anyone else's screws.

US. Is that it?

HIM. Yes.

US. Okay! We will call you if we're going to buy.

We wondered if any other computer companies could convince us to buy their brands, so we tried Toshiba.

US. Why should I choose Toshiba over its competitors?

TOSHIBA. That's a good question . . . (*After pausing and trying unsuccessfully to think of an answer*) What are you going to be using it for?

US. Basic usage, emailing, Internet, office apps, etc.

TOSHIBA. I'm going to tell you straight up, they are all similar.

US. So is there anything that makes Toshiba a better brand? Something that would make me choose it over its many competitors?

TOSHIBA. Well, all of the components inside our computers are made by Toshiba. If you open up another company's computer, it will have parts made by all different manufacturers. If you look inside our computers, more of the parts are actually made by Toshiba.

US. Other than its Toshiba guts, what else would make me want to choose a Toshiba computer?

TOSHIBA. We have completely free 24-hour service if you have any problems with your Toshiba computer. Free for the length of your warranty, which is typically one year. And the nice thing is, if anything goes wrong with your computer, we send you a box, you pack it up, we pay for shipping costs and fix it for you. Also there is an international warranty.

US. Is Toshiba better for any specific programs/tasks—i.e., gaming, graphic design, etc.?

TOSHIBA. It depends on which programs you will be using, and what system they are designed to run best on. I'm not going to say Toshiba is the best. (*After some pushing and prodding*) Durability. The hard drive immediately stops spinning on impact, preventing information loss.

You will notice from this exchange that the salesperson identified some features and benefits that are interesting. In other words, there was some substance in this conversation, as opposed to the generalities and banalities that characterized so many of our other phone calls, and not just with computer companies. We don't know if those features and benefits are unique to Toshiba or if it is just the only company that articulated them, but what was still missing from this conversation was a sense of who Toshiba is and what it stands for, and why that is beneficial to me.

Why is that important if Toshiba's computers have some cool features and benefits? Because they are easy for other companies to copy, if they haven't done so already (or if Toshiba didn't copy them from someone else). The moment another company shares the same features and benefits, you are forced to default to a price battle, which is the hell that most companies want to avoid at all costs. Yet they constantly drive themselves to price wars through their own behaviour.

Outsourced Sales Agencies

Next, we spoke to presidents of sales agencies. These are companies you can outsource your sales function to if you don't want to or can't do your own sales for whatever reason. We thought these would be great companies to call because, as experts in sales for their customers, they should know how to sell themselves, right?

Wrong!

One president answered the question "Why should I choose you?" with two words: "Our customers." This is a standard response, and as a sales support point, it is useful. To be able to point to name-brand customers as an indication of your credibility is powerful. However, it isn't a primary point of differentiation. Your customers aren't what make you uniquely remarkable; what you do for your customers that nobody else can do is what makes you uniquely remarkable.

We asked him what it is about his customers that made them the reason we should choose him. "They're happy." We told him that the other agencies we talked to have happy customers too. He told us he would call us back on Monday with an answer.

Lo and behold, the call came on Monday. Even with the weekend to consider, he couldn't come up with a compelling response as to why we should buy his services. He essentially reiterated his answer of the previous Friday, going over the details of how happy his customers are and why that is a reason that we should hire his company for our sales outsourcing needs.

Why would you hire someone to do your sales if they can't sell themselves? If they can't sell themselves in a clear and compelling way, that means they won't be able to sell your products effectively, right? Not necessarily, but it makes you wonder. You shouldn't, as part of your sales process, be creating this uncertainty about your ability to deliver.

Banks

We phoned a branch manager and told her we were going to open a business account. We asked her why we should open the account and begin a long-term business relationship at her company and with her branch. Her answer was refreshingly honest. She said that all banks offer essentially the same services and that hers simply did them better. We asked her to explain to us how, specifically, her bank does them better so that we can feel comfortable choosing her branch. Rather than answer our question, she suggested we try the other banks and, once we did, she was confident we would see the difference and come back to her branch.

When you actually think this suggestion through, it is quite absurd! First of all, unless you had a specific reason to do so, you would never have business accounts running at four or more different banks simultaneously. So to follow through on her suggestion, you would have to go to a competitive bank, open an account and, in all likelihood, stay with that bank for at least a year before you got a sense of the quality of its service. After that year, you would close that business relationship and start a new one with another competitive bank for about a year. You would have to do that again and again until you had spent many years sampling all of the major banks (assuming you restrict your purchase decision test only to major banks). After five or six years, according to her suggestion, you would now be in a position to make your decision as to what bank you were going to choose for your long-term business relationship. And when you make that decision, you would choose her bank because you will now know, from firsthand experience, that her bank does exactly the same things as every other bank, only better.

Or she could just make things simple for us and tell us, in a clear, concise and compelling way, why we should choose her bank. Let's look at how some other banks did, starting with Citibank.

us. Why should I choose Citibank?

CITIBANK. We have many different options: loans, chequing/savings accounts, Thank You Rewards system . . .

US. Well, all banks have a variety of options. What is it that makes your bank better than any others?

CITIBANK. Friendly staff 24 hours a day who will provide details to fix your account, financial information.

US. What's to say the next person I call won't be so friendly? How can I be sure to get such service here and not elsewhere?

CITIBANK. It's our job. We scored top in a customer survey for our friendly service.

US. So I'm not sure I want to count on customer service, since other banks claim they have the best customer service, too. Is there another reason I should choose Citibank?

CITIBANK. The catch here is that Citibank is well known. We have worldwide banking, so anywhere there is a Citibank, you can ask questions, and customers can always contact us.

We were then transferred to a personal banker.

US. Why should I choose Citibank?

CITIBANK. Well, Citibank is worldwide.

US. So what would you say is the reason to choose Citibank and not another?

CITIBANK. Um, I guess just the access worldwide.

Citibank does have a lot of great services, no question about that. And it is worldwide, which is beneficial to many people. So it can tell us what it does, but what it can't do very effectively is explain why that is useful to us. Let's see if Wells Fargo can do any better.

us. Why should I open an account at Wells Fargo?

WELLS FARGO. We have lots of different accounts and services. We offer bill-paying services, free cheques, online and phone access. And Wells Fargo has the best customer phone service that is still available on holidays, and a text-messaging service to notify customers when they overdraw on their account.

us. What would you say is the best thing about Wells Fargo?

WELLS FARGO. The telephone and online banking and bill-paying service online or over the phone.

us. But what differentiates Wells Fargo from all other banks?

WELLS FARGO. Numerous different products. You can get insurance for your car, home, health and even your pet. Mortgages and loans.

us. Other banks offer those services too. So the one thing to set Wells Fargo apart from other banks is . . . ?

WELLS FARGO. It's all in one.

That last part—"It's all in one"—wasn't a preconceived idea. She arrived at this conclusion as a result of the conversation. We got that a lot—people making stuff up as they went along. Remember the Dell guy? We don't think "our screws are stronger" was ever a part of Michael Dell's sales script, nor would it ever be in the future.

Canada is the only Western country that didn't have to give its banks a single penny of bailout money in the global economic meltdown of 2008–2009. Does the secret of their success include the ability to differentiate? We already looked at one bank's sales approach at the beginning of this section ("try everyone else and then come back to us"). Let's see what a different bank had to say.

us. Can you tell me why I should choose you as my bank?

CIBC. Surely. Our customer service is at the top of other banks. (*He claimed there are surveys to prove this, but we know all of the*

banks can "prove" their customer service is the best.) We offer product mixes to serve you best and maintain service fees that are competitive. (*He provided an example of their free cheques—or rather, cheques included in the $12.95 monthly cost.*) The fees in the long run will catch up to you. With no free cheques at other banks, there are long-term costs. There are hidden fees at other banks.
US. So what does CIBC do better than other banks?
CIBC. Well, it delivers what matters . . . to your expectations . . . and tailored to your particular needs.

Money plays a very intimate role in all of our lives. It either enhances or inhibits virtually everything we do. So when you're in the business of providing and managing money for your customers, it means you play an intimate role in your customers' lives. Selling on the basis of "our fees are a fraction lower," "we answer the phone when you call" or "we have a wide range of services to suit your needs" doesn't come remotely close to capturing the importance of the role a bank plays in the lives of its retail customers.

Two Serious Problems in Almost Every Organization

In each of these examples, you could argue we got the wrong person on the wrong day at the wrong company. While this is true in theory, the reality of our experience is that we talked to over 100 companies, from the biggest of the multinationals to small entrepreneurs, and not one of them could give us a clear and compelling answer as to why we should choose them over their competitors.

One of two serious problems exists in all of these examples. Either the company doesn't have a compelling answer to the question "Why should I choose you?" or it does but the answer can't, for some reason, permeate its way throughout the organization. How can this be? We know many of these companies as some of the biggest, most sophisticated and successful companies in the world, yet they can't answer a question as basic as "Why should I choose you?"

Should they care, especially if they are making sales? Should *you* care? There is one compelling reason why you should care: it makes sales come faster and easier.

ACKNOWLEDGEMENTS

This book would not have been possible without the pushing, prodding, encouraging and tough love of our friend Howard Lichtman. After we spent two years trying to get the book started, Howard said to us, "We're going to get this thing done . . . *now!*" He dragged us up to his office once a week for three months to pound out the first draft with the patient help of his assistant, Lori Neumann (thank you, Lori!). The book has taken many twists and turns since that summer, but without Howard's commitment to us and his big heart, you wouldn't be holding this book in your hands today.

Howard's other great contribution to this book was introducing us to our amazing agents, Victoria Skurnick and Jim Greenberg of Levine Greenberg in New York. We will be forever grateful for their commitment, patience and determination to us and this book. Every time there was a setback, they found a different path to getting the book published. Their substantial role in the creation of this book is humbling.

Brad Wilson was our champion inside HarperCollins. For 18 months, he guided us newbies through the process of writing, editing and promoting this book. His passion for our book was obvious and encouraging, and he had many great ideas to contribute but was never pushy in how he presented them. Thanks also to Noelle Zitzer, the managing editor at HarperCollins, for her support and to our eagle-eyed copyeditor, Lloyd Davis, who somehow managed to catch every dangling participle, split infinitive and subject/verb disagreement.

We are indebted to Jaime Watt and Michael Burns, the two members of our advisory board, who have given us invaluable advice, direction, mentoring and support over the years.

We would also like to thank all of the clients we worked with over the past ten years. Every one of you took a leap of faith when you agreed to participate in this unorthodox process. Many of you have become lifelong friends and even strategic partners, which we cherish. You were an integral part of an exciting ride for us and the learning in every single Blueprint was instrumental in the constant evolution of the Blueprint process.

Finally, we would like to thank you for reading this book. We spent almost half a century each, directly and indirectly, developing the Blueprint process and its underlying philosophy. We are very passionate about what we've developed and what we do, and we are grateful to you for reading this book and becoming a part of our journey.